JAN 92
91
90
MAR 89 MOVED IN HERE
MAR 88
87
MAR 86 2nd apt.
truck MAR 86 1st apt

951-2397

THE $2 WINDOW ON WALL STREET

Other books by Ira U. Cobleigh

THE $2 WINDOW ON WALL STREET

Ira U. Cobleigh
and
Peter J. DeAngelis, CFA

MACMILLAN PUBLISHING COMPANY

NEW YORK

COLLIER MACMILLAN PUBLISHERS

LONDON

Macmillan Publishing Company
866 Third Avenue, New York, N.Y. 10022
Collier Macmillan Canada, Inc.

Library of Congress Cataloging-in-Publication Data

Cobleigh, Ira U.

The $2 window on Wall Street.

Includes index.

1. Speculation.   2. Stocks—United States.

3. Wall Street.   I. DeAngelis, Peter J.   II. Title.

III. Title: Two dollar window on Wall Street.

HG6015.C76   1986   332.63′22   85-23690

ISBN 0-02-526480-X

Macmillan books are available at special discounts for bulk purchases for sales promotions, premiums, fund-raising, or educational use. For details, contact:

Special Sales Director
Macmillan Publishing Company
866 Third Avenue
New York, New York 10022

10 9 8 7 6 5 4 3 2 1

Designed by Jack Meserole

Printed in the United States of America

Contents

Preface

This title was borrowed from race-track parlance. The $2 bet is the common denominator at every horse park and conjures up expectations of big payoffs on small stakes. We have used the $2 Window to refer to stocks on Wall Street that are available at very low prices—often at $2 or less, but including those below $10.

The same race-track expectations of quick riches are epidemic on Wall Street. Millions of people are constantly scanning the quotations of lower-priced stocks hoping to pick out one that may multiply tenfold. There's a thrill to it. Indeed, if you speculate on Wall Street, you should never be bored. You'll be too busy watching the price changes in your portfolio of hopefuls!

There also are differences between betting on a horse race and gambling on a "long shot" stock. With the horse bet, it's almost always pure luck, and there is little information you can gather that gives any assurance of a winning selection. In stocks, however, you can get useful facts from corporate reports and news releases that may tell you when a company is improving, when its profits are rising, or that people are rushing to buy its shares.

Further, in horse playing, the result is known within three minutes. Either you've won a hatful or you've lost

little factual information

your stake forever. With a $2 stock, however, even if it sinks almost to zero, you can hang on and wait for a better day when it may become a market darling. You're almost never wiped out. Even if your "dog" languishes for years and skirts bankruptcy, it may stage a remarkable comeback. Hundreds have!

We probably have overworked this analogy between gambling and speculation. Of course, the money involved in stock is larger. You will need at least $200 (100 shares @ $2) on Wall Street against a $2 minimum horse bet at the track. But we do want to stress the eagerness of millions to make swift killings in stallions or stocks. Our aim is to show how you can score impressive gains on a small capital outlay by observing a few cardinal rules in stock selection. We feature, in particular, our own Operation BaitBack, designed to pin down your profits and to prevent them from melting away like butter in the noonday sun.

Your quest for riches in $2 stocks is no wild goose chase. It is based on logic and history. In addition to the much-heralded, legendary $2 Window successes, such as IBM, Xerox, Polaroid, and Digital Switch, we also will cite lesser-known $2 successes of recent years whose stock prices have gained sensationally. All of these stocks traded at one time below $5 a share, and all later generated capital gains of 2,000 percent or more! There always are rich opportunities lurking among the long shots. It's up to us to direct you to them, and we will present current-day $2 Window candidates for your consideration.

A main reason for writing this book is that the whole field of low-priced stocks has been neglected for so long by the professionals, because of their speculative risks, thin markets, and the availability of only meager statistical information. The major stock-exchange firms provide splendid research on seasoned blue-chip stocks, such as Exxon, American Brands, IBM, or Atlantic Richfield. A leading firm may regularly track and report on 1,200 companies, but not one of their recommmended stocks will sell as low as $2 a share! These $2 stocks have been studiously ignored and overlooked by the large investment firms.

That gives us a broad, open field for our work—many promising low-priced stocks begin at $2 or lower and may go as high as $10. The success of cellar speculation is based on price leverage. A long-range observation of market action reveals that under normal trading conditions a stock quoted at $50 is twice as likely to double as one selling at $100; a stock at $20 is in line for a higher percentage gain than one quoted at $50; and a stock at $5 should advance, on favorable news, at a much faster rate than one at $10. However, this also is true in reverse. In sharp declines, the bids for little stocks will melt faster than those for highly capitalized seasoned shares. While there are high risks in this market section, they are offset by higher rewards.

Accordingly, we say speculate, don't gamble, and don't become compulsive about doing either! Don't risk the rent money or Junior's college fund on a paddock favorite or a market long shot! Be an informed speculator! Know something about each stock you buy and have a good reason for every buy or sell decision you ever make! This way you provide some insulation against tragic loss, and you greatly improve your prospects for winning.

Enough, however, of this philosophical discussion. The purpose of this book is to demonstrate that low-priced stocks have potential speculative merit. In fact, some of the most rewarding and elegant blue chips of the affluent today were once neglected bargains at the $2 Window. A low-priced stock is designed to give you plenty of action—and a

constant tug-of-war between hopes and fears. If you speculate in the basement of corporation finance, your pastime is
certain to add zest to your life and, with good fortune,
money to your purse.

There are now 42 million stockholders in America. At
least 8 million of them are long-shot speculators at heart,
far more interested in "making a killing" than collecting
dividends. No practical road map has heretofore been available to them. These speculators have been given little en-
couragement by major brokers and only a minimum of
available research. Hundreds of potential fortune-building
stocks right now are trading at $5 or below. We propose to
provide a road map identifying some of them. It is still
possible to make a killing on Wall Street among researched
low-priced stocks! So read on!

Acknowledgments

While we have taken a number of years to synthesize the ideas in this book, they never would have gotten between two covers without the help of friends and associates. Among those to be acknowledged are our colleagues—past and present—within the investment community who monitor financial events in that arena daily, especially our close associate, Kevin V. Theiss, whose counsel and guidance have been invaluable in thinking through many of the basic ideas in this book. Kevin has been a collaborator in every phase of development from conception through numerous drafts.

We also owe a large debt to many corporations cited whose successes have rewarded their shareholders handsomely at the $2 Window.

Barbara Mysko and Christine Onoszko are to be especially thanked for their patience and faultless typing and retyping of the manuscript. Margaret DeAngelis especially is acknowledged for her support, and for her reading and rereading of the manuscript, which has resulted in much wise counsel and contribution.

Of great assistance were the computer systems and expertise of Conner Capital Corporation of Summit, New Jersey. Utilizing their computers enhanced the speed of some operations and made others feasible.

Finally, a special acknowledgment to M.C. Horsey & Company, Inc. of Salisbury, Maryland for providing the stock price charts presented.

THE $2 WINDOW ON WALL STREET

1

The Popularity and Profitability of Low-Priced Stocks

Since August 1982 there has been a solid uptrend in the stock market, not heard since the late 1960s. On August 3, 1984, a record volume of trading was reported on the New York Stock Exchange—an amazing 236 million shares on a single day, and the Dow Jones Industrial Average has reached a new high of 1537.61 with no downturn in sight. The documentation of market popularity was the motivation for this book. We believe that the United States is entering the second leg of a major bull market that will carry the Dow well past 2000 in the coming year and attract millions of new "players."

In 1984 inflation was stifled, General Motors earned more than $6 billion, and stock buyers, avidly following the daily quotations, exceeded $42 million. New entrants are steadily attracted, in particular, as they set up and expand their Keogh and IRA investment programs.

The comparison of 1984 with the late 1960s deserves further comment. Nineteen sixty-eight was the last meaningful year of a bull market before inflation set in. There were 25 million stockholders, and the great majority of investors then owned their shares outright (in full, not on margin). Speculation was well controlled, with the margin rate at 80 percent (a far cry from 1929, when there were fewer than 2 million stockholders, and they could, and did, speculate madly with only 10 percent down).

The excesses of 1968 were not in highly leveraged "shoestring" trading, as one might expect, but in the exalted price/earnings ratios of glamor stocks (P/E ratio is the ratio between the current share price and its net earnings for the latest 12-month period). Computers and nursing homes were selling at sixty times earnings, as was Avon. Control Data rose to $156. Minnie Pearl Fried Chicken went public at $20 and hit $40 on the offering day. During 1967–68 Wang Laboratories soared from $12.50 to $87. Investors should have been warned that many of these prices were too high, because the Dow Jones Industrial Average, even at the top of bull markets, has never sold above twenty times earnings.

Another feature worth noting about the 1968 and earlier bull markets is that lower-priced shares were generally ignored and did not normally attract a popular following until the market headed for its cresting or explosive phase. We thus conclude that the 1984–86 market cycle should offer excellent opportunities in cellar stocks, as investors prepare to move down in price ranges, looking for shares that haven't had their move. The older a bull market, the more new speculators are attracted to its lower-priced stocks, including droves of those too timid to enter earlier.

The climate today appears promising for the speculative program we favor. We suggest that investors with sporting blood set aside 10 percent of their portfolios for a program of stocks at the $2 Window. But don't gamble with the rent money! Also, if losing money in the market makes you ill, this program is not for you! There will be risks and losses, and giddy, speculative swings to ride out. On balance, however, you can win a bundle if you're both lucky and informed. And you can have fun!

How to Be Your Own Security Analyst We have assembled a series of procedures that should work well. First of all, you must be informed: Have a good reason for every buy and sell decision you make! Don't buy on tips, hearsay, gossip, or just because some smart aleck at a cocktail party boasts that he's making a killing in Zilchboom Electronics! Select a customer's broker at a stock exchange firm, but don't expect him to provide recommendations on low-priced issues.

It's beneficial to do current reading about the stock market. Read the financial pages of a major metropolitan newspaper; select a financial journal such as *The Wall Street Journal, Barron's, Forbes, Financial World,* the *Market Chronicle,* or the *OTC Review.*

Also, get as much information as you can from brokerage houses on lower-priced stocks they may track, or from their research reports or market letters. Your shopping list is massive. There are thirty or forty $2 stocks listed on the NYSE below $5; hundreds on the AMEX; a universe of penny shares on the Spokane, Vancouver, and Toronto stock exchanges; and thousands of issues trading Over-the-Counter.

The larger issues are tabulated regularly in newspapers in their daily NASDAQ (National Association of Security Dealers Automated Quotations) sections, but the actual market for most can best be gleaned directly from a broker/ dealer who actively trades in low-priced stocks. He probably subscribes to a financial service that publishes daily "pink sheets"—a list of quotations of bid-and-ask prices on thousands of issues, ranging from such exalted equities as

DeBeers Consolidated Mines (world's largest diamond dealer) to a hopeful gold mine stock like Pegasus or Stan West Mining. Stocks not quoted by NASDAQ may be found listed in the pink sheets, and an up-to-the-minute quote may be gotten from a broker.

Some of these lesser-known companies may be featured in *Barron's, Financial World, OTC Review*, or summarized in Value Line or Standard & Poor's reports. Once you know the name of the company that interests you, the best step is to request the latest annual report, quarterly report, or press releases directly from the company's headquarters. You'll find the company listed in a Standard & Poor's corporate directory at your broker's office or a library. If a company is not listed in such a directory, don't be shy, call a broker with a firm making a market in that stock. Any stockbroker can identify the market-making firms for you.

There also are several hundred new stocks issued each year by companies going public. Many of these are offered at $5 or below. Get a prospectus from one of the underwriters listed in the newspaper ad that announced the offering. You often can do well by buying at the offering price if a company is legitimate, if it has good products and services, significant real-estate or mineral assets, and if it is offered at a reasonable price by a reputable firm or syndicate. But beware of the many new issues that are overpriced, of development-stage operations with no grounds on which to assess value, or of outright turkeys!

No matter where you get your information, however, here you must look for.

1. A company that is operating in an uptick or turnaround industry. There is no point, and rarely any profit, in

fighting a downtrend, a mature market, or a nongrowth business.

2. Evidence of near-term profitability and a clear potential for future rising earnings' power.

3. A situation that holds some special attraction that may stimulate an eager market following; for example, a technological edge, a patent, a special process, an innovative or proprietary product line, or a special service. Companies whose products and/or services are breakthroughs frequently become stock-market sensations (Tampax, Syntex, Tropicana, Cardiac Pacemakers, McDonald's, H & R Block's Tax Service, Century 21 Realty chain, and many more, all waxed great on fortune-building innovations). Here the investor must take extra care not to be swept away and misled by a fad masquerading as a trend. For those readers of the older generation, no hoola hoops! For those of an envious younger generation, no video-game stocks!

4. The presence of hidden assets. Such run the gamut from a tax-loss carry-forward to undervalued real-estate holdings, from operating divisions or subsidiaries that are collectively worth far more than the present stock-market value of the whole to grossly undervalued "hard assets," or from potentially significant injections of cash from nonrelated business sources to dormant business sectors poised for rebirth.

5. Proven skills that should be evident among top management either by a track record of previous business successes or by the company's present operating history.

6. The viability of the company as a takeover candidate. If the subject company is established in a desirable industry, it is often the object of attention of larger corporate

suitors. Typically, the capital cost of entry for a new-comer in an industry, compounded by marketing uncertainty, makes it more advantageous and less risky for a firm to "buy in" via an out-and-out takeover or joint venture arrangement. The acquired company usually is acquired at a handsome premium over its prevailing stock-market price, which more than likely already has enjoyed a major upward move. An example cited earlier in this chapter is Cardiac Pacemakers, the pioneer in lithium-powered pacemakers. After a phenomenal rise in the price of its stock, Cardiac Pacemakers was acquired by Eli Lilly and Co., at a substantial premium, as well.

Brokerage Firms We have mentioned the previous sources of information because regular brokerage channels may not provide what you need. Big brokerage firms don't like dealing in stocks below $5 and even have set up roadblocks against them: (1) they generally research only a few hundred stocks, almost never those below $5, and seldom volunteer a report on a small Over-the-Counter issue; (2) they deny margin on stocks below $5; (3) they may ask the customer to sign a statement explaining that he has bought the stock unsolicited and not on the basis of any recommendation by the firm; (4) they often will not accept an order for stock below $5 or may deny a commission to the customer's broker who receives the order; and (5) they may require a higher commission rate at the $2 Window than on higher-priced stocks. However, they will execute any order to sell, even the worst dog!

The reasons for these various roadblocks are defensive. The firm may be afraid that either the customer will bring suit if his low-priced shares decline and cause heavy loss or he will blame the firm for "putting him in" such risky shares. Further, it is as costly to handle payment and transfer of a $2 stock transaction as a traditional seasoned issue, which the firm may recommend, and the commission to the firm is lower.

Most firms feel that they will best maintain a customer's account, and goodwill, by suggesting mature stocks with broad markets that the firm has researched. Firms following a know-your-investor policy have decided that low-priced stocks have no proper place in well-managed portfolios. Finally, brokerage houses, in recent years, have added many new brokers to their staffs. Some of these newer representatives may lack the knowledge or experience to counsel clients in the trading of risky low-ticket shares. However, recent Security and Exchange Commission decisions have indicated that brokers are obligated to supply accurate and current information to clients on securities in which they may trade.

We mention all of these things only to stress the fact that you may have to comb the market yourself in order to identify $2 stocks of promise. We provide some excellent guidelines later in the book, plus a diversified list of hopeful speculations in many sectors: mining, electronics, real estate, petroleum, financial service, and technology.

There is a cluster of winners moving toward a crest awaiting only your prudent selection and timely purchase.

THE MARKETS, WHERE THEY ARE TRADED

In order to trade any class of securities from penny stocks to government bonds, it is essential to have a marketplace where issues are regularly bought and sold. The ideal market is one in which the trading is active, the spread between bid and ask is narrow, the daily volume is substantial, transactions are promptly reported, and records of sales and/or bid-and-ask prices published daily on financial pages. The largest markets are in government bonds and in the stocks of major corporations with outstanding shares counted in the millions.

New York Stock Exchange   The best-known market, worldwide, is the New York Stock Exchange (NYSE). It is the habitat of shares of leading industrial corporations, banks, railways, airlines, utilities, natural resources, and consumer and service organizations. About 2,300 stock issues are listed on the NYSE, and total volume of shares traded runs at the rate of 80 to 100 million shares daily. Peak activity was on August 3, 1984, when 236.6 million shares changed hands. The NYSE deals for the most part in higher-priced stocks, and 70 percent or more of the trading volume is generated by institutions. There are relatively few shares on the NYSE at $5 or below, and purchases by individuals are mainly among the blue-chip stocks. The Dow Jones Industrial Average, composed of thirty diversified major-company shares, all listed on NYSE, is the accepted stock-market barometer. The NYSE is not a primary hunting group for $2 Window opportunities.

American Stock Exchange   The second major exchange is the American Stock Exchange (AMEX). Here the patronage is mainly by individuals. The shares listed are generally of smaller, less-seasoned companies than those listed on the NYSE, and AMEX prices are in the lower ranges. The AMEX is $2 Window turf. You will find dozens of issues, some of substantial merit and promise, quoted at $5 or less. The activity, volume, and volatility of the AMEX, and the diversity of companies and industries represented make the American Stock Exchange a major trading arena for readers of this book.

Regional Exchanges   Smaller, regional exchanges in the U.S. include The Midwest in Chicago, The Philadelphia-Baltimore Exchange, The Boston Stock Exchange, The Pacific Coast Exchange. These may trade in issues listed on the NYSE after that market has closed, but are mainly devoted to making markets in the securities of companies operating in their geographical regions.

At the bottom of the exchanges are those in Vancouver, in Denver, and in Spokane, which specialize in penny and promotional stocks, mainly of early-phase exploration mining companies or development-stage enterprises. These penny issues may have millions of outstanding shares. The lure here is quick action and great price volatility. It is not uncommon for a mine share "on Vancouver" to double in value in a single trading session, particularly in the lowest price ranges. Active trading easily can push a 5¢ share to 10¢ without any change whatever in the condition of the company just by a rumor about it! Speculation in mining shares is very risky, because often such securities lack any visible merit, or assets, or significant ore body. These markets are often boldly manipulated by unscrupulous brokers or operators, and shares are touted in hyped-up market letters or so-called research studies. These markets are fanned by ignorance, since the average long-shot speculator has no capacity to evaluate the grades, extent, or potential of alleged mineralized areas or claims described in company reports or releases.

There is considerable speculation by Americans in the securities of Canada. There, the major exchanges are in

Montreal and Toronto; smaller ones are in Edmonton (featuring hopeful oil companies) and in Vancouver (already mentioned)—a hotbed of metal-mining shares.

Over-the-Counter All publicly traded shares on exchanges are "listed"; those not on exchanges are called "unlisted" and are bought, sold, and quoted "over the counter." The Over-The-Counter (OTC) market is actually the largest because it includes the trading of most government securities, corporate bonds, preferred stock, and the common shares of about 14,000 banks, as well as many important insurance companies.

In the stock sector of this OTC market, there are about 20,000 issues traded or quoted with some frequency. Perhaps 7,000 of these will be tabulated in the daily pink sheets published and distributed by The National Quotation Bureau. In these pink sheets each issue is set down in alphabetical order, and opposite it is listed the broker or brokers "making a market" in it. Making a market describes the willingness of a broker to bid on or to offer a stock for immediate purchase or sale. Brokers may list their best bid or ask price, or merely show BW (bid wanted) or OW (offering wanted). These markets are made either by independent OTC broker/dealers in various cities across the country or by the OTC trading departments of stock-exchange firms. OTC trades are either "as principals," where securities are owned or purchased by firms "for their own accounts," or "as brokers," charging a commission for each transaction.

Trading Trading on the exchanges is done by auction, with each transaction concluded by competitive bidding, conducted by a "floor broker" who is the designated "specialist" in one issue or more. The function of the specialist is to maintain an orderly trading market in the issues to which he has been assigned, and to stand "at his post" (one of dozens of trading booths on the floor of the exchange) ready to make a bid or offering price for shares, regardless of the state of the market or the absence of other buyers or sellers.

The major distinction between exchange and OTC trading is that markets on the exchanges are made usually by a single specialist, whereas in OTC many dealers may make competitive markets in the same issue. Hundreds of corporations have preferred the multiple market in OTC for a broader-based commitment to creating liquidity.

Except in the most active issues, spreads in OTC trading are wider than on the NYSE or AMEX, mainly because they are thinly traded. So defend yourself and watch the spreads. The "inside" spread between bid-and-ask prices, which you find in daily financial sections, represents the highest current bid and the lowest available offer available among a network of broker/dealers across the country. You must consider this spread, because the wider it is the more your stock must move for you to break even when you sell. One way to proceed is to put in "limit orders." Place your limit "at the opening," above the bid and below the offer. Then wait. Chances are by the end of the day some broker will get itchy, narrow the spread, and "hit" your bid. But keep your order in for one day only. Don't go away on a trip with limit orders hanging around!

Scan volume. If it and prices are rising day-to-day, don't defer your buying. Don't enter an order so big that it rocks the price. A transaction of more than a quarter of prevailing trading volume is enough to jolt the market in the average OTC stock. Remember that with small companies and high transaction costs, your risks are higher. Don't buy to catch intermediate trading savings. If the stock doesn't offer the prospect of gaining 50 percent in six months, don't buy it!

NASDAQ   In recent years important refinements have been made in OTC trading. Before 1971, traders made markets and executed orders, mainly with brokers listed in the pink sheets, over the telephone. It was fairly expensive and often time-consuming, and market timing could be lost because of overcrowded wires on trading desks and delayed long-distance calls.

In 1971 The National Association of Security Dealers introduced NASDAQ. NASDAQ is an electronic system instantly listing volume and price of the last transaction and providing bid-and-ask prices at the punch of a button on actively traded securities. This NASDAQ trading has displaced the pink sheets in market making in the more actively traded issues of the larger corporations. There are now over 475 NASDAQ-listed companies divided into three groups when published daily in *The New York Times*:

1. NASDAQ National Market;
2. NASDAQ National List; and
3. NASDAQ Supplemental OTC List.

The first classification, National Market, covers the actively traded issues of larger capitalized companies, like Apple Computer, MCI, Intel, Noxell, and large regional banks. The National Market tabulates dividend rate (if any) and volume of sales for the preceding day, high, low, and last quotation. The recently organized National Market System offers, in addition to the traditional multiple market makers, complete and instant reporting of transactions. The second group, National List, tabulates only dividend rates, volume, and closing bid-and-ask prices. The Supple-mental OTC List records bid-and-ask prices only.

NASDAQ quotes are supplied electronically when a given trading symbol is punched on a console in a broker's office. NASDAQ is constantly improving its efficiency and gearing up for 100-million-share days.

More than 600 companies now trading on NASDAQ qualify for listing on the NYSE, and over 1,800 qualify for the AMEX, yet they remain in the OTC sector because of preference for multiple-trading markets. OTC contrasts with a single specialist on an exchange. Minimum qualifications for NASDAQ listings are $300,000 in annual earnings or $8 million in net worth.

For active trading issues, NASDAQ has replaced the pink sheets. NASDAQ provides easy access to market information both by daily summaries appearing in the financial press and by instantaneous data supplied by computers, covering over 1,000 companies.

For our purposes most of the stocks we seek are traded either on the AMEX or OTC.

The Markets The foregoing outline of markets seemed appropriate, because in placing orders for the purchase or sale of securities, you should be mindful of the breadth and kind of trading in each issue under consideration. On the NYSE you have broad markets with large daily volumes, so the best procedure is usually to buy or sell "at the market." The AMEX market is not so broad, nor is the volume as high. OTC transaction markets are thinner, and there are wider spreads between bid-and-ask prices. Some OTC stocks may have as little as a million shares outstanding, closely held, with only 400 or 500 stockholders and a "float" of only 300,000 shares. Here your order should be at a price, and you may have to wait hours or days for it to be filled. In general, we prefer the broader markets for low-priced speculation, because after purchase you want plenty of players around when you decide to sell! In dull or declining markets particularly, OTC bids may be thin and may recede swiftly against any sizable offering.

Your trading results should definitely be improved by your knowledge of the distinctions between the various trading markets. Favor the exchanges for prompt executions, transactions reports, and closer markets—narrower spreads between bid-and-ask prices.

Stockbrokers   About brokers. Our own preference is for the established, full-service exchange houses. These provide not only reliable quotes and executions and impressive solvency, but extensive information and research reports useful in making timely decisions about securities, companies, or industries. There also have appeared in recent years several discount brokerage houses that merely execute your orders and charge less because they do not offer the other services.

Whichever way you decide, make sure that the firm you deal with has substantial capital resources and is certain to make delivery of securities purchased, or held in safekeeping, when you request!

WINNING STOCKS AT THE $2 WINDOW

The logic behind this book is that there are always ample fortune-building stocks waiting at the $2 Window. The case for carefully selected low-priced stocks has splendid documentation. In recent years, as in the past, those issues that have racked up the greatest percentage gains were ones that started out well below $10, and in many cases, under $5 a share. There are, however, pitfalls, and we advise the speculators to seek out exclusively the special situation as opposed to random speculation. A special situation is a stock that offers great potential reward with a low or negative definable risk. That is, a "heads I win, tails I don't lose" reward/risk feature. The speculation offers great potential reward but with much risk. Remember, you can afford to be selective, since you only need to parlay relatively few of these winners to achieve the windfall pinnacle. Like most of the good things in this life, there is a catch. The catch is that an effort is required by the investor to investigate each potential $2 Window stock selection and ensure that key investment criteria are met before taking the plunge and placing a bet. Investing on whim or superficial information occasionally may be successful, but in the long term is doomed to fail.

Facilities should be available to you at stock exchange firms or small but reputable brokers/dealers through whom you can acquire reports on lesser-known companies and the industries they serve. The information available to the investor is, in Wall Street jargon, in the public domain and is more than sufficient to identify performing candidates. Do not place excessive reliance on the research of security analysts in major Wall Street firms. All the information you require is available under law to the investment public at large in press releases and in quarterly and annual reports.

We have prepared case histories of four companies in which early speculators who held on "made it big." In each instance it was possible to have bought a stock at or below $5 a share and made a killing on as little as an initial investment of $1,000. These stocks, unlike the legendary IBM's, and Xerox's, are lesser-known companies that have achieved their amazing successes only in recent years. They are real-life success stories and ones in which your authors have been involved, in one form or another, during development stages and spectacular stock price moves.

In each of these cases, you will observe that there were three major elements in the corporate success: solid management, unusually rapid growth rates both in the company and the industry served, and dynamic earning power. Of these, the most important is the last. Over the long range, stock prices will move in direct proportion to their current earning power, giving promise and expectations of rising future earnings. Not only does a stock price typically reflect the gains in earnings, but as a history for profit growth is compiled, the price/earnings multiple of the subject stock usually expands as well, producing a geometric improvement in price quotations. When selecting a stock for gain always keep in mind the race car driver's motto, "What's behind me is not important—it's what's in front that counts." The powerful propulsion provided by expanding earnings is the key to success.

Mylan Laboratories Inc. (MYLN) [OTC] In 1976, Roy McKnight and Mike Puskar, recognizing the growth of and need for quality generic drugs, took over the reins of a small and financially troubled publicly-owned generic drug company. At that time the company, Mylan Laboratories, was losing in excess of $1 million annually on just under $14 million of revenues. McKnight and Puskar assembled an able management team, provided intermediate financing from their own pockets, and implemented administrative and growth programs for the company. Within a year financial integrity and profitable operations were restored. However, it was not until two years later, in 1978, that an earnings growth trend became evident. By 1980 sales had almost doubled to more than $22 million, and Mylan had become the leading independent generic drug company in the United States.

Today sales have again more than doubled to over $53 million for the fiscal year ended March 31, 1985, and net earnings have soared since 1980 from $630,000 to $12.5 million. The company's product line—encompassing more than twenty-five different drug categories including antibiotics, analgesics, diuretics, and tranquilizers—is sold internationally. It is particularly noteworthy that after five years of research, Mylan received FDA approval for its patented new drug Maxzide™, a diuretic antihypertension product, which competes directly with SmithKline Beckman's Dyazide®, the nation's most widely prescribed drug. Thus, Mylan Laboratories has grown in less than ten years from an obscure, financially troubled company to become a leader in its industry today by having developed its own new pharmaceuticals to compete effectively with the drug giants.

As spectacular as its financial and operating record is, it pales in comparison to its stock-price performance. The authors first became aware of the company in 1977 and have followed this stock's rise from the equivalent of 12½¢ a share to its 1985 high market value of $26—nearly a 17,600 percent gain! A mere $1,000 invested in 1977 and held to early 1985 would be the equivalent of 8,000 shares, or at market prices $176,000! Never mind that you didn't invest in 1977. There was ample opportunity to observe the progress achieved and make an investment as late as 1980, when an impressive record had been compiled, financial strength achieved, and future prospects were bright. In 1980 the stock traded at 37½¢—a mere triple that of 1977! Nevertheless, were an investor to have waited until 1980, his gain would have been in the area of 6,000 percent at today's prices. A laggard investor awaiting further evidence before making this investment would have parlayed $1,000 into more than $88,000 in only a four-year period!

Of course, at the time the stock was not a penny stock. It sold at the $2 Window for a price under $10. It has since been the beneficiary of numerous stock dividends and stock splits—six, to be exact. There are presently approximately 24 million shares outstanding, which typically trade in volume—hundreds of thousands of shares a day. Here, then, is a latter day stock success so dramatic that it rivals the Wall Street legends such as Occidental Petroleum and Teledyne. Most impressive is that the company continues to look forward to years of outstanding earnings' growth in the area of perhaps 30 percent annually. Mylan Laboratories is living proof that the $2 Window offers up amazing opportunities.

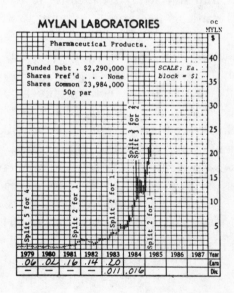

MYLAN LABORATORIES

Pharmaceutical Products.

Funded Debt . $2,290,000
Shares Pref'd . . . None
Shares Common 23,984,000
50¢ par

SCALE: Ea.
block = $1

	1979	1980	1981	1982	1983	1984	1985	1986	1987	Year
Earn	.06	.02	.16	.14	.20					
Div.	—	—	—	—	.011	.016				

Dranetz Technologies, Inc. (DRAN) [OTC] Another relatively unknown success story is Dranetz Technologies, Inc., formerly Dranetz Engineering Laboratories, Inc. Founded in the early 1960s, with an initial public offering later that decade, this northern New Jersey company, exceptionally strong financially, manufactures precision electronic instrumentation equipment for computer service organizations, electrical power companies, and producers of communication equipment. Its products serve a need perceived early and met by its founders, Abe Dranetz and Irv Backinoff. Dranetz Technologies' superior products have established the industry's standards of excellence and are the driving force behind its, not surprisingly, rise from an obscure, small, nominally profitable company of less than $2 million in revenues ten years ago, to one with revenues approaching $30 million and net earnings last year of $4 million.

The company's operating progress is matched by its phenomenal financial strength. Unheard of for a company its size, Dranetz has built and maintained a financial statement that would be the envy of a company many times its size. Cash and equivalents alone total approximately $10 million and its balance sheet is debt free. Trading Over-the-Counter, this stock first came to the authors' attention as a *Dowbeaters*® choice in May 1978 when it sold at 5¾. Adjusted for subsequent stock dividends and splits, the price has risen from the equivalent of 50¢ a share to a 1983 high of more than $18—a 3,600 percent capital gain. Even at today's prices, its shares, which now provide a 15¢ cash dividend, represent a 2,600 percent advance. A $1,000 investment in 1978 would have appreciated to a maximum of $36,000, or would have a present value in today's market of $26,000!

Today Dranetz Technologies has outstanding approximately 5 million shares. It still trades OTC under the symbol DRAN. Its stock is held in prestigious institutional investor portfolios and is a classic example of a rewarding growth stock at the $2 Window.

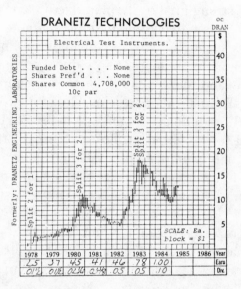

Telecom Plus International, Inc. (TELE) [OTC] Industries emerge and evolve in various manners. Most progress from an orderly development of a product or service, while others are born of technological advancement and/or some special need. However, some industries, and subsequently companies, are literally created by the legislative pen. The 1968 Supreme Court Carterfone decision brought into being, overnight, an industry that has grown from a zero base since that time to a multibillion dollar business today. What the Carterfone decision did was to permit independent companies to manufacture and market telephone equipment heretofore supplied only by Ma Bell. Specifically, this historic decision allowed non-AT&T companies to sell private branch exchanges (PBX's) and related systems directly to individual customers. Subsequent legal decisions removed legal and regulatory obstacles of the telephone industry and opened the doors to the private, independent telephone companies and suppliers. With the establishment of the new telephone market, there also emerged many significant companies including Telecom Plus International, Inc. (formerly Telecom Equipment Corp.). Telecom began life anew when a management team, headed by Stephen R. Cohen (now chief executive officer), entered in the mid-1970s and assumed control in March 1976. The company, formerly plagued by an erratic record and indecisive management, with corrective action, was able to stabilize and position itself as a beneficiary of this burgeoning industry.

This rapidly expanding company has moved from a sales base of less than $2 million in 1975 to more than $155 million in 1984. Telecom sells, installs, and services telephone equipment systems through fifty-three regional facilities in the mid-Atlantic, New England, Gulf Coast, Midwest, and southern California as well as in Puerto Rico. The major portion of Telecom's revenues is obtained through the sale of computer-controlled branch-exchange (CBX) telephone systems designed for a broad range of businesses and institutional users. The company has installed and serviced the facilities of many of the Fortune 100 companies and today stands as an undisputed leader in its field.

Growth has been achieved through internal as well as external (acquisition) means. The stock, since 1978 selling at a low of $1, adjusted for stock splits, has appreciated to a high of $16 and at this writing trades at $11, representing a

1,100 percent gain. Telecom has more than 23 million common shares outstanding and trades Over-the-Counter. It is a clear and proven winner at the $2 Window, where $1,000 could parlay to $11,000.

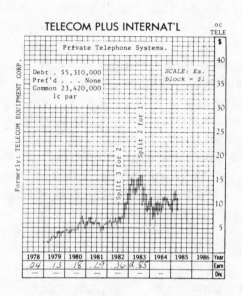

Kulicke & Soffa Industries, Inc. (KLIC) [OTC]   Today the acknowledged U.S. leader in the design, manufacture, and sale of precision equipment, instruments, and tools used in the production of semiconductor devices, Kulicke & Soffa was, in the late 1970s, only a modest sized and cyclical company with an erratic record. By September 30, 1984, sales reached a new high of about $120 million with net earnings of $14.1 million. [Kulicke's products are state-of-the-art and advance the industry standard.] Its product line includes assembly machinery, such as manual, semi-automatic and automatic wire and die bonders, and consumable micro-tools used on certain of the company's or its competitors' machinery. Approximately 70 percent of sales are now represented by wire bonders, of which the company is the world's leading producer. The stock, as with most growth companies, has been the subject of numerous stock splits. Traded Over-the-Counter there are now about 7,400,000 shares outstanding. Having reached its current prominence, institutional holdings total approximately 50 percent. In 1977 and 1978 Kulicke sold at approximately $1 to $2 a share. It subsequently rose to 34¾ in 1983. A $1,000 investment in 1978 held to early 1985 would've produced a $20,000 value, or a 2,000 percent capital gain, or even much more, had the investor been agile enough to sell near the higher price. In the above commentary we are by no means suggesting that KLIC has stopped growing. Today's technology is bound to continue to call upon this company's product and services, and KLIC seems destined to prosper.

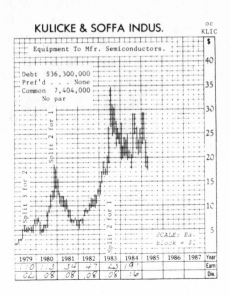

KULICKE & SOFFA INDUS.

SUMMARY

There you have it—four virtually unknown companies that have produced extraordinary profit for the $2 Window investor. One a health-oriented company participating in the needs of the changing giant pharmaceutical industry, another serving the rapidly changing and growing communications industry and, finally, two high-technology companies carving special niches for themselves. While the companies reviewed are in quite diverse business sectors, their success and rewards to early investors depended on a number of factors they had in common, namely, the essential ingredients of quality standards, imaginative management, innovative research, effective marketing, and excellent financial planning and controls.

2

Investment Strategies

This book subdivides $2 Window stock selections into three categories: trading range, revival or special situation, and growth stocks. Successful trading positions for trading range and revival stocks should be centered on the expectation of a 50 percent gain at least within 15 months and ultimate sales creating capital gains, not ordinary income. These objectives must be clearly in mind as you make each market decision. We see no sense in frequent in-and-out trading because no one can gauge or anticipate accurately daily swings; further, a lot of rollover transactions will erode profits through excessive brokerage commissions.

Before you buy, have some assurance that the stock you select has a reasonable prospect for rapid gain and will not "just sit there" like a tired toad or go down. You must have two things going for you in low-priced shares: the overall trend of the market, and favorable or improving conditions for both the company you choose and the industry it's in. If the market climate is not right, your chances of gain are lessened. It's fun to be "in the market," but to enter, or hang in, if the trend is visibly bearish may prove painful.

Growth stocks, on the other hand, require different treatment. If the company you select is a "baby Xerox" and gaining in sales and profits at a rate of better than 30 percent a year, be in no hurry to sell, and almost never for less than a 100 percent gain. So watch the quarterly reports, and as long as the rapid growth you identified when you purchased your shares continues or improves, it will pay you to maintain your investment.

Your program should not be limited just to a series of purchases and sales (including occasional sales at a loss when you bought a turkey). Have some mature, long-term investment in mind into which you can siphon off and salt away a percentage of trading profits. Consider, for example, taking a third of your winnings each year and putting them into a well-managed, open-end fund such as Tri-Continental Corp. or Lehman Corp., or a good closed-end mutual stock fund such as Scudder, Dreyfus, or Fidelity. This way you will have the zest and profit of speculating while building your net worth and a dependable second income for later, possibly retirement, living. So many people make a lot of money in their lives but have nothing to show for it because they either overspend, fritter away profits, or have no organized program for building a mature investment portfolio.

TRADING RANGE STOCKS

As noted, one means of successful deployment of your speculative dollars in low-priced stocks is investment in trading-range stock—shares of companies that seldom move dramatically in their levels of business or profits, but swing in cycles over several years. Obviously, a speculative procedure in these issues requires market agility. In this chapter we outline useful procedures in these more volatile shares, some with yo-yo characteristics; that is, they move up rapidly, then plummet erratically, often with little warning. These trading-range stocks generally enjoy active daily markets with good volume.

Success in these trading range shares involves a selective winnowing out of those companies with dull or negative horizons or of those industries going nowhere or downhill. Screening the values in the-lowest market sector depends not so much on the industry as the "numbers" and prospects of particular issues.

Earlier evaluation systems first required identification of an industry in its expansion phase, and then selection of a likely winner from companies in the group. Often the second-largest company was preferred, perhaps because as No. 2 it had to "try harder." That system ignored price range, however. The No. 2 stock might sell at $40 a share and thus not qualify for our book.

Unfortunately, no such pat formula is available to us. Instead, our low-level procedure may begin by scanning transactions on, say, the American Stock Exchange or the Over-the-Counter market on a day selected at random, noting those stocks selling at $5 or below. From this group we may select the ten most actively traded issues (greatest daily volumes) that ended the day on an up-tick. The purpose of this exercise is to identify issues attracting the most players. An animate following is a valuable guideline to a performing stock.

Activity or sponsorship may be generated by rising sales earnings, profits or expectations of such, or by emotional factors.

Such "mob psychology" reactions may be to: a merger or acquisition rumor, a novel product or entry into a new market, a hopeful lawsuit, a breakthrough patent or technology, a spinoff, or a change in management. A rumor doesn't have to be well-founded to generate market velocity.

Indeed, many stocks go higher simply because they have already advanced! Market momentum is often as likely to create fat near-term trading profits in your stock holdings as record earnings!

To illustrate this psychological response, a few years back there was a mania for citizen band (CB) radios. Everyone from truck drivers to hot-rod fans to Volkswagen buffs had to have a CB in their cars to communicate with other CBs! Every "handle" was greeted with "good buddy." A company called High Gain Electronics Corp. swiftly became a leading maker of CBs. Its shares were avidly sought as the demand for these new electronic gadgets seemed infinite. High Gain moved from 50¢ to $24 in two years. Along the way there was a public offering at $19! Nimble traders made killings as they unloaded on the way up. The fad died suddenly, and High Gain thudded back to 50¢—all within three years.

This is a classic example of the volatility in low-priced trading range stocks and demonstrates that market agility may be more helpful in this form of speculation than skillful security analysis.

Another illustration comes to mind, this time from the boom in precious metals, 1979 to 1980. In 1979 the commodity markets were awash with speculation in silver and gold. Rumors of "a corner in silver" were spread, based on reported buying by the infamous Hunt brothers. Zeal for silver spilled over into the stock market, and Hecla Mining, a leading silver producer, caught the fancy of the players. Hecla rose in 1979 from 4⅝ to 45½. It was the leading gainer for the year on the NYSE. Silver itself soared from $15 an ounce to a high of $48.80 on January 19, 1981. Then the bubble burst and silver fell back to $15. Hecla, too, dived and hit a low of 13⅜ in 1980. Another magnificent market yo-yo, creating fortunes for those who sold before the crest and anguish for those who lingered on.

It has always been a lot easier to make money on Wall Street than to keep it. Whole generations of speculators learned that lesson in 1929, 1969–70, 1974, and as recently as mid-1982. These examples are cited to warn of the pitfalls of "distribution" markets. Active trading range stocks generally go through four states: accumulation, markup, distribution, and liquidation.

1. ACCUMULATION. When shares are scraping bottom after progressive liquidation.
2. MARKUP. When perceptive buyers already have been buying and propel the market into an up cycle.
3. DISTRIBUTION. When the market nears a cyclical crest and the shrewd and the agile investors unload.
4. LIQUIDATION. When the most adroit traders have exited, sellers outnumber buyers and the market gains downward momentum toward bargain levels, and it dawns on the multitude that they've hung on too long!

Discern, if you can, the current phase of the shares you may be considering for purchase.

This all leads up to the purpose of this chapter: generating gains in trading-range issues. Dozens of companies whose shares are quoted below $5 today have never (or seldom) sold above $10. Yet these companies remain in business even though their profit records are erratic or nonexistent. These stocks are unlikely to soar, but gaining 100 percent or losing a large fraction of their market value within two years is a common occurrence. Timely trading between these price extremes can be rewarding and a lot of fun. But it requires market agility and scanning trends in prices and trading volume in the issues you own. Watch also quarterly earnings reports and press releases about issues acquired or those you may be considering. Your selection of low-priced trading range issues is wide. It includes oil and mining shares; tired or troubled companies; small technology, medical products, or service companies. There are always new arrivals, new issues, reorganized companies, and spinoffs.

You will note we have repeatedly stressed trading volume. This is important because you cannot afford wide spreads in low-priced issues. The spread is the gap between bid-and-ask prices and typically is characteristic of a small capitalization or thinly traded particular stock. Specifically, a large spread would be, by way of example, a stock with a bid (offer to buy) of $3 a share and ask (offer to sell) of $4 a share. Assuming that you buy at the bid and sell at the offer, you must now have a gain of 33 percent to break even. Here, the broker, market maker, or specialist takes the easy money, or "cream," with the result of sharply reducing your opportunity for gain. Finally, you want to be certain of a broad market activity (volume of shares traded) so that when it's time to sell you can do so in an orderly manner. Market liquidity is of prime importance. The absence of such will assure an inactive market with large gaps and thin trading volume. Unless such a stock is a remarkable bargain, you'll do well not to invest in it, because of poor liquidity.

REVIVAL STOCKS

You will recall that in the Bible there is mention of a man named Lazarus who was raised from the dead. A lot of stocks, devastated by disaster, insolvency, or bankruptcy, also come back to life, almost miraculously, usually by a reorganization, but sometimes merely by the injection of new capital or a timely merger at the last minute. In fact, often the only chance at corporate life for some companies is first to die (Chapter 11 reorganization).

The Great Depression was replete with languishing securities. Corporations went into bankruptcy by droves, banks failed by the thousands, real estate and mortgages were foreclosed, and over one-third of U.S. railway mileage went bankrupt. Four-thousand banks closed their doors in 1933. This set the stage for amazing opportunities for capital gain.

At the depths of the Depression, in July 1932, Anaconda Copper sold at $4, down from $138 in September 1929; Montgomery Ward at $4, down from a $138 high; Blue Ridge at 63¢, down from $24; General Motors $8, down from $73; United Founders 50¢, down from $117—and these were solvent companies! Total disaster befell Associated Gas & Electric, Middle West Utilities, Bank of United States, Kreuger & Toll, and Insull Utility Investments.

Fortunes were made, especially in defaulted and reorganized railway securities from 1933 to 1940. Many railway shares—New York, New Haven, and Hartford; St. Louis, San Francisco; Chicago, Rock Island and Pacific; Chicago, Milwaukee, and St. Paul; and Boston and Maine shares sold below $2 at some time, and yet all scored dazzling comebacks via reorganization.

Some Winners   To illustrate, in reorganization Chicago, Milwaukee, and St. Paul became Chicago, Milwaukee Corporation. While it was in Chapter 11, operating under court order, the company sold off several parts of the railroad, a lot of timberland, and paid off its bondholders. From all these divestitures and very prudent management, the company became cash-rich, and the shares rose from a low of $4 to $176 a share, in August 1984. Some comeback!

The reorganizations of Boston and Maine, and Rock Island were also ultimately rewarding. New shares of Chicago Pacific Corporation (survivor company of Rock Island) zoomed from $5 to $81 since the reorganization in 1979.

Another classic example of revival is Toys "R" Us. This toy-store chain was spun off from the bankruptcy of Interstate Stores in 1978. The Toys shares moved from 75¢ a share then to $52.75 in 1984, all from the ashes of insolvency.

More recently, Manville Corp. took a dive into Chapter 11 in 1982. It wasn't actually bankrupt, but the company faced thousands of lawsuits, totaling in the billions, from individuals whose health had been impaired by asbestos, manufactured by Manville. It entered bankruptcy to achieve consolidation and lump-sum settlement of all those claims and to return to normal operations without this albatross around its neck. At the time of entry into Chapter 11, the shares sold as low as $4, from a $46.25 high, and represented a speculative opportunity. The stock has since risen to $13.62. The company has not yet settled its lawsuit claims, but it has been earning profits and has substantially enhanced its working capital in the interim. Dividends are accruing on the preferred stock as is back interest on the bonds.

We do not wish to assert that emergence from bankruptcy is always rewarding. Many businesses do not survive but are liquidated for so many cents on the dollar for creditors, and common stock may be wiped out.

Some Losers   A nonwinner of insolvency is Braniff International. The airline was overcapitalized and had some high-priced labor contracts. It entered Chapter 11. It got a "white knight" early in the proceeding: The wealthy Pritzker family of Chicago came along and agreed to take control and to supply millions to bring the property back into operation. Speculators foolishly bid up Braniff shares to $6.50 in hopes of a brisk turnaround. The reorganization plan, however, introduced a new company, Dalfort Corp., which offered one new Dalfort share for each 125 old Braniff shares. But Dalfort stock started trading (OTC) at only $36 a share after the exchange offer, which valued old Braniff common at a measly 30¢! A restoration of partial operations developed, the company limited its flight schedules and sold off major landing field rights.

On October 26, 1984, another airline bit the dust. Air One, the first air transport aimed exclusively at business travelers, filed under Chapter 11. The company started out in January 1981, after the industry deregulation, and in April 1983 began service out of St. Louis with nine Boeing 727's. It offered first-class service at coach prices, but couldn't fill the seats. Other carriers, TWA and Ozark, provided stiff competition on routes to Newark, Washington, and Los Angeles, and by October 1984, Air One had lost $42.2 million. It had expected a substantial investment by Southern Express, which was not made. The shares plunged from a high of $6 to 35¢ a share in late October 1984. This situation may be worth watching, but is obviously extremely hazardous.

Lionel Corp., traditional maker of toy trains, went into bankruptcy, and its shares rose from 50¢ to $5. Pending sale of its 62 percent interest in Dale Electronics, Lionel realized enough to keep the business going and returned its operations to the black.

As this was written, Baldwin United and Charter Company, both identified with sale of single-premium annuities, are in Chapter 11. One or both may get bought out by a solvent insurance company. But the situations are complicated, and future profit potentials or market recovery are difficult to define.

A major bankruptcy, not without promise, was that incurred by the Wickes Corp. Here was a merchandise retailer grossing $3 billion that ran out of working capital. The shares sold as high as $47.25 but trade currently at $3. Here a scale-down in operations restored profitability, and the company enjoys a huge tax-loss carry-forward. These shares have an active market, and the picture appears to offer some promise. In 1985 the company received a substantial injection of new capital in the form of "junk bonds."

We have cited some examples of troubled securities. There are also companies that only skirted bankruptcy, but later on rewarded patient shareowners rather well. Lockheed Corp. was on the ropes a few years ago when the U.S. government put up the money to keep it going. Lockheed actually sold at 7/8 at its worst, but recovered miraculously, gaining over 3,500 percent from the low to a high!

Then what about Chrysler? It hovered at the brink until the government advanced more than a billion dollars, a transfusion that made Chrysler the most sensational recuperator in history. The stock moved from a distress low of $3 to a 1984 high of $44.25. Imagine, in the first nine months of 1984, Chrysler earned $13.97 a share!

Chapter 11 and Reorganization   The point we have been making is that tottering and wheezing companies often present remarkable opportunities for speculative gains. But you need four things to win: information, vision, timing, and patience. Indeed, some of these sick shares can make a lot more money for you than stocks with sturdy balance sheets and unclouded solvency.

Consider the basic assets of a company, particularly valuable land such as chain-store or fast-food-restaurant sites. Also, consider the value of any patents or franchises. Important, too, is the industry a company is in and the opportunity for acquiring a better management, or an acquiring company, to take over. Review the latest annual report and note if some losing divisions can be sold or liquidated or uneconomical branches closed. In most big, established companies there is usually a lot of executive "blubber" as well as a percentage of slovenly employees who can be declared redundant. Cutting payrolls is standard procedure for reviving languid corporations.

While a company is under court orders, it may default on interest payments, eliminate dividends, renegotiate leases, restructure labor contracts, and take many other steps calculated to build up cash and to restore solvency. All the while the property is in Chapter 11, the stock may drag along the bottom, allowing time for accumulation at "fire sale" prices. The best time to buy threadbare shares is usually when a company enters Chapter 11, or soon after. That's when investors give up, and panic selling is rampant. The odds favor speculators in shares quoted at panic levels. They've gone as low as they could.

Next comes the plan of reorganization; this must be scanned diligently. Note what percentage in new securities goes to bondholders and to general creditors and, in particular, the terms under which old stockholders may exchange their holdings for new shares. Watch out for dilution. Relate the exchange offer to the prevailing price of old stock and note (if available) the new stock's (when issued) trading range. Arrive at some estimate of total asset value for the restructured company, and try to calculate a reasonable appraisal value for the new shares. Get some idea of possible earnings per share for the next twelve months. Also, look for a tax-loss carry-forward. This is usually a big item in a reviving company. It means that the new corporation will not have to pay taxes on any profits for some time (often years) ahead. Further, a tax loss is most attractive to a highly prosperous possible acquisitor.

No amount of study or research can guarantee you a winner in these revivals. No two bankruptcies are alike. But some fundamental analysis is certain to be helpful. Patience is also essential. Once a company goes bankrupt, investors shun it, and months may be required to rebuild market recognition and sponsorship for the reorganized shares. Look at Chrysler. It sells today at 2½ times earnings just because people remember that it was once a pilot test for a financial Forest Lawn!

Later in this chapter we will leaven our advice by referral to some companies now in the financial doghouse that you may want to consider as long shots. For those who do not care to make their own decisions in these troubled waters, there are some mutual funds and some investment-advisory subscription services that specialize in building portfolios out of bottom-rung securities. A few that come to mind are: Phoenix Fund (sponsored by Merrill Lynch); Investor's Discovery Fund; Mutual Shares Corporation; and a unique and prominent company, The Hallwood Group, selling at $1 a share on the NYSE. Their portfolios may reach into other borderline situations: nuclear power companies like Public Service of New Hampshire, Long Island Lighting, and Consumers Power; technology stocks that have almost run out of gas; or, as in Hallwood, tired real-estate trusts. The whole field is exciting, and fortunate, timely selections can pay off handsomely.

GROWTH STOCKS

The characterization "growth stock" is certainly one of the most frequently used, misunderstood, overdefined, and abused terms on Wall Street. Too often it is quickly applied to what a friend, Robert Hannon, chief executive officer of Boonton Electronics Corporation, refers to as a "flash stock." He and the authors of this book look upon some of the antics of the financial community with amusement and frustration, as we witness the lemming-like rush to ill-defined growth industries. To the previously mentioned citizens-band-radio and video-game fads, one could easily add other now-abandoned recent darlings such as the personal computer, energy-generating windmill, CAT scanner. To be sure, many of these businesses can and do fall back to a maintenance level, but they never become growth areas. Rather, this type of stock may well fall into the earlier discussed trading-range stock category. Here they are treated as they should be; namely, as pieces of paper to be bought and sold under strict discipline and within relatively short time horizons.

A growth-type stock is one of a company that advances on the basis of steady rises in sales, profits, and corporate stature. Growth, as the name implies, is synonymous with continuity, innovation, substance, expansion, and strength—in other words, staying power. These are fundamental attributes. You must push aside the hype to clearly identify a growth stock. Look at the four summarized examples in Chapter 1 of $2 Window growth stocks that made it. Measure them against the criteria for selection presented in the preceding chapter, and you have 90 percent of the battle fought in identifying a low-priced stock of a growth company. However, that last 10 percent is much like the final yard in a touchdown—it's vital! Here it is the stock's price action and market conditions. That final ingredient, combined with the analytical screening out of the growth company, makes for a potentially powerful equity.

There are fashions in finance just the same as there are fashions in apparel, motor cars, art, or literature. In the 1950s the fashion of growth stocks emerged, and a cult of devotees sprang up among analysts, portfolio managers, and well-heeled individual investors who were less interested in cash dividends. Indeed, the 1950s represented the golden age of corporate growth, with government bonds yielding three percent, the world rebuilding after a massive war, a climate of peace, no inflation, and an upsurge in production of goods and services in the United States.

Some fabulously rewarding growth stocks blossomed in the 1950s: Columbia Broadcasting, Transworld Air, Admiral, Xerox, Franklin Life, G. D. Searle, and 3M, for example. Early entrants into these equities made fortunes just by hanging on, because they advanced spectacularly. In-and-out, short-term trading in such issues was not a good tactic. It was more rewarding to await the flowering of earnings and stock dividends to multiply one's shareholdings.

Growth stocks of stature continued to surface in the 1960s and to attract strong followings until the market crested in 1968. In this period, the star performers included Kentucky Fried Chicken, McDonald's, Sheraton, Occidental Petroleum, Perkin Elmer, and Control Data.

Fashionable growth stocks seemed to fade in the 1970s, as oil prices zoomed and U.S. inflation set in as an after-effect of the war in Vietnam. In the intervening years, other factors softened the demand for growth stocks. These included the advance in technical analysis and the rising popularity of mutual funds. These funds employed new procedures for portfolio management due to their need to display and record significant capital gains each year. One feature of these procedures was accelerated trading. It was no longer popular to sit with a stock for five years (a reasonable span for the maturing of a growth issue). Instead, portfolios were systematically rolled over, so that today there are dozens of mutual funds with a 100 percent turnover of their portfolio assets each year. Even staid pension and endowment funds in 1984 reported average turnovers of more than 50 percent. With that kind of management by professional investors, and their competitive urge to outperform, stress was placed on market velocity and timing rather than on patient retention while awaiting share prices to reflect expanding earning powers.

After this brief review, we would like to reaffirm the historic virtues of growth stocks and the zest in buying a low-priced stock at $2 that trebles and splits in a few years. Growth stocks, you will recall, along with recovery and trading stocks, were set forth as our chosen areas for winning speculations.

Growth stocks relate to aggressive companies in expanding industries. They are not easy to select. Even in sectors of great technological advancement and high profitability, many newcomers will fall by the wayside. In 1905 motor car manufacture represented the greatest growth industry in history. In this century there have been more than 900 motor car companies launched and more than 2,000 makes of cars produced. But how many survivors? Only four: Ford, Chrysler, American Motors, and General Motors, the classic growth stock of the century. What ever became of the Moon, Velie, Dort, Dorris, Metz, Pierce Arrow, Jackson, Franklin, and Stanley Steamer?

A growth company must first document its capacity to survive and then expand its sales and profits at an inordinate rate. An early position in a dramatic new industry is just not enough. There has been, however, a magnificent succession of amazing winners as new technologies and methods have emerged in television, space, drugs, computers, fast foods, insurance, pacemakers, discount retailing, and travel. Our task is to identify up-and-coming companies in the forefront of the future.

Where shall we look? Fiber glass, computer software, video cassettes, cellular radios, space weaponry, packaging, waste disposal, jails for profit, genetics, financial services, birth control, computer banking? Keep on the lookout for new industrial opportunities. Make sure there's a real future ahead, not just a fad like CB radios, hula hoops, Nehru jackets, or snowmobiles.

The $2 Window growth stock provides the greatest opportunity for gain over a longer period of time, but unlike its brethren, the trading-range and revival stocks, it requires constant surveillance to make certain the company remains on track operationally and the stock's price doesn't outpace itself. The moment a company's growth prospects show evidence of lessening, or its stock price becomes the questionable object of the financial community's fancy and moves beyond any sane P/E—it's time to depart and take profits! One of the early warning signs is when your formerly low-price pick becomes recognized by Wall Street or, more specifically, institutional investors, large brokerage-firm analysts, and the financial press. Of these, most infamous for their late entry, promulgated excesses, and panic exits are the institutional investors—which incidentally are believed to account for three-quarters or more of the New York Stock Exchange market activity.

Wall Street's fickle treatment of growth-stock favorites is legendary. Yesterday's sweetheart is literally dumped, and woe to the shareholder who stubbornly holds on or fails to recognize the clear evidence of stock price excesses. Often he or she loses not only the paper profits but possibly

some of the initial investment. It has happened to us all—
authors included! For that purpose, Chapter 7 is dedicated
to the art of selling and pinning down profits. We stress the
subject here so that readers, when considering a low-price
growth stock, will also include in their investment strategy
the art of timely selling.

After identifying an upbeat industry, you will want
some guidelines for the selection of superior growth stock
within it. Here's a good check list to add to those funda-
mentals presented in Chapter 1.

The company selected should evidence:

1. an industry growing 50 percent faster than the economy;
2. sales of at least $5 million a year (to assure survival);
3. high and rising profit margins (net profits rising faster
than sales);
4. sales expansion of 15 percent or more a year—rapid and
consistent;
5. a return of 20 percent on stockholders' equity;
6. more than 600 stockholders, to assure marketability,
with small or minimal institutional stock holdings (a
growth stock should be bought before it is big enough
to attract institutions).

Growth stocks should be bought in their early stages.
Avoid paying too high a P/E multiple—preferably below
twenty times. A fair multiple may be the growth rate. Also,
be sure that there is a good "floating supply" of stock.
Finally, for our purposes, the stock should be priced below
$10, preferably way below.

Growth stocks are acquired for long-term gains, not in-
and-out trading. You may have to wait three years for a
growth issue to fulfill its promise, and your ultimate objec-

tive should be a gain of at least 200 percent. Don't expect dividend income since these expanding equities seldom pay out more than 20 percent of net profits; but do expect stock dividends, stock splits, and rising P/E multiples to enhance the value of your holdings.

Teledyne Inc.   It would be difficult to cite a better long-term growth stock example over the years than Teledyne Inc. From the investor's viewpoint, here is the record. The stock commenced trading in 1962 at $2 a share. It closed at $23 in 1967, $129 in 1982, and traded as high as $274 in 1985—a golden performance.

Teledyne was one of the early conglomerates, starting operations in 1961 and earning 1¢ a share on 6.4 million shares in that year. Founded by Henry Singleton, the current chairman and CEO, Teledyne named George Roberts president, in 1966. Together this team has brilliantly managed a portfolio of diversified companies and rewarded its investors with impressive capital gains.

Today Teledyne is comprised of more than 130 autonomous and independent companies in a wide diversity of businesses. Its operations are in four major sectors: industrial (36 percent of 1983 sales), aviation and electronics (35 percent), specialty metals (20 percent), consumers products (9 percent). The industrial output is in gasoline and diesel engines for tractors, military vehicles, construction, and materials handling machinery. Aviation includes turbine engines, air vehicles, electronic and avionic systems. Teledyne produces all major commercially important metals and alloys for use in industrial and utility plants, in aerospace, and in cutting and drilling components.

Teledyne has a substantial group of unconsolidated subsidiaries in insurance companies and equity positions in

6

Bargains in Basement Stocks

In earlier chapters we highlighted the speculative merits of low-priced stocks. We cited several issues that swiftly built small stakes into fortunes and outlined winning procedures for identifying issues that promise superior market performance. It is time to convert that assorted wisdom to successful trading in today's markets.

If you are now ready to invest at the $2 Window, then consider some of the issues we have researched and described. They are, naturally, low-priced, they enjoy active markets, they are widely diversified and include all three categories we listed earlier: trading-range, revival, or growth-type stocks. Trading-range transactions should strike pay dirt within a shorter time period—six to twelve months; revival stocks, possibly longer; and growth shares may take as long as three years for rising earnings to be reflected in broader market sponsorship and higher P/E multiples.

Your success will depend on the selections you make based on then current earnings, balance sheets, management records, technical charts, and the stage of the whole market. Timing is vital! It is much more important to buy cheap than to sell dear. When your stock has surged ahead and it's time to sell, refer to the special chapters in this book on when to sell. This will give you amazingly helpful guidance on cashing in and when to use Operation Baitback— our own procedure for selling using the proceeds of sale to reduce the cost of remaining holdings to zero. After that you ride on velvet!

We also want to stress diversification. Speculation in basement stocks should be spread over three to five issues. That way risks are shared and one turkey can't wipe you out. Refer also to the instructions given earlier on how to place your order in various markets so that you can enter a situation at the lowest cost and not pay through the nose, say, for a thinly traded OTC issue.

With these points in mind, we suggest that you now consider the following group of stocks we have screened. Because of the inevitable time lag between the writing of this book and its publication, changes, of course, will have taken place in the earnings, market price, and prospects of each issue. Some shares may have advanced out of prudent buying range; others may be less attractive in view of altered conditions; but most should still be at a level of opportunity. Good luck!

GROWTH STOCKS

Microsemi Corp. ($5½: OTC–MSCC) Microsemi designs, manufactures, and markets high reliability diodes and transient voltage suppressors for military, industrial, and medical applications. The company is the second largest independent producer of diodes in the United States. With the acquisition of the zener diode division of Siemens Corporation, MSCC more than doubled its sales and is now one of the largest producers of zener diodes in the world.

Major products of Microsemi include glass and plastic bonded diodes, glass and plastic bonded transient voltage suppressors, and rectifiers and temperature compensating devices. The company produces the only glass diode qualified for the Joint Army-Navy Space Program.

In recent years MSCC has widened its market share via a solid promotion effort. Also it has been a beneficiary of an industry shakeout, since larger manufacturers have been unable to compete effectively against a highly specialized company such as Microsemi. Historically, the company has had an active acquisitions program. Product lines were acquired from Centralab Semiconductor in 1975 and Teledyne Semiconductor in 1979. The 1982 acquisition of the Siemens division adds greater penetration in plastic diodes and plastic transient voltage suppressors supplying industrial and the rapidly growing computer markets. All domestic production of plastic devices have been consolidated at the former Siemens plant in Scottsdale, Arizona, resulting in a major profit turnaround. Semcon Electronics Ltd. of Bombay, India, has attained profitable operations after MSCC increased its ownership in 1983 to 100 percent from 20 percent. During 1984, MSCC continued its acquisitions with the purchase of two commercial lead axial rectifier product lines from the International Rectifier Corporation. Microsemi's corporate headquarters are located in Santa Ana, California, with additional manufacturing facilities in Scottsdale, Arizona; Hong Kong; and Bombay, India.

Microsemi is achieving greater market penetration, and new markets have opened up for its transient voltage suppressors. These sophisticated devices, which prevent external voltage from entering into circuits, are vital to key items, such as pacemakers, and other sensitive equipment, such as personal computers. These two markets alone represent a large potential. Additionally, the highly reliable glass diode produced for the Joint Army-Navy Space Program has received greater-than-anticipated nonmilitary orders.

The diode market is in excess of $1 billion annually, a very large percentage of which consists of captive producers manufacturing for their internal requirements. The independent market is dominated by only a handful of companies of which Microsemi is now the second largest. Microsemi could exceed the 20 percent annual industry growth with its active acquisitions program and as its market share continues to expand.

Total corporate sales have increased at a compounded rate of more than 40 percent from $2,682,000 in 1977 to $30,278,000 in 1984. Income from operations has grown even more dramatically from $220,000 in 1977 to $4,767,000 in 1984. Net income has increased correspondingly from $163,000 in 1977 to $2,717,000 in 1984. Sales and net income for the fiscal year ending September 30, 1985, are projected at $35 million and in excess of $3.9 million (approximately 52¢ per share), respectively. There are outstanding common and common equivalent shares of 7.8 million. Microsemi, a clear winner as a corporate entity, has yet to become a recognized winner in the stock market. Selling at the $2 Window for 5½, MCSS appears an imposing value.

Scanforms, Inc. ($2½: OTC–SCFM) Scanforms is another attractive low-priced value. Scanforms is engaged in the design, printing, manufacture, and sales of personalized computer letters used in direct mail applications, and continuous forms, primarily specialty forms and optically scanable forms. Specialty forms are used principally for advertising and promotion by the direct-mail marketing industry. The company is one of only twelve such firms in the United States capable of producing foil-embossed, multicolored direct-mail marketing material. Recent investment in new state-of-the-art equipment has enabled Scanforms to offer a complete variety of services, including an ability to allow the customer to effect changes midstream in design and material.

The firm's design and production capabilities are augmented by a small, impressive, effective national marketing program. The marketing effort is carried by nine internal sales representatives primarily covering the eastern seaboard and some outside brokers in the Midwest and throughout the nation.

Scanforms is a leader in direct-mail advertising for the growing population of armchair shoppers in this country. This industry has grown in size and variety to a level where it is estimated by trade sources that market expenditures for direct mail now approach, if not exceed, $20 billion. To be certain, the industry is segmented, and the segment in which Scanform's particular market lies totals approximately $250 million and is increasing at a 25 percent annual rate. The industry is also highly fragmented. The number of firms involved is large and their size small. Consequently, Scanforms is a major factor in its industry segment by virtue of its multimillion-dollar revenues and its unique design, production, and specialty capabilities. As such, the company holds promise of not only growing with the industry, but achieving greater market penetration.

Scanforms is a classic revival situation. The company history is one of first recovering from the verge of bankruptcy in July 1977 and then progressing to pretax earnings of $1.3 million in the fiscal year ending September 30, 1980, on sales of $7.1 million. However, Scanforms soon after encountered the combined problems of (1) a deepening economic recession, which impaired sales; (2) a union organization drive, which was defeated; (3) heavy investment in new equipment, which laid virtually idle for some time due to the retrofit by the manufacturer to meet performance specifications; and (4) a shift from dealer sales to direct sales. The result was a setback which, while not as severe as the company's earlier difficulties, nevertheless produced net losses for the fiscal years ending in September 1981 and 1982 fiscal years of $400,565 and $987,874, respectively.

Twice reborn from its difficulties, Scanforms now turns in a profitable growth mode with a leaner corporate silhouette. The client list of the company, which was maintained during these difficult periods at admittedly lesser volume levels per client, is now expanding in volume per client as well as in the addition of new clients such as American Express, Prudential, All-State Insurance, *Business Week*, *Who's Who*, and *National Geographic*.

Evidence of the turn is now apparent in figures for the fiscal year ending September 30, 1984. Sales rose 26 percent to $11,496,303 and net earnings rose to 16¢ per share on 3,163,460 shares outstanding versus the prior year's 11¢ per share. It is estimated for the fiscal year to end September 30, 1985, the company sales will reach record levels of $13 million with net earnings per share of about 13¢. Importantly, the breakout in earnings is expected to commence in the following fiscal year with preliminary forecasts placing sales at $16 million and net earnings per share of 25¢.

Scanforms also has broken new technological ground in its field. Scanvelope is a recent product development receiving strong marketing response. Scanforms now has the ability to print multicolor material on continuous forms, *breakout*

perforating, folding and inserting the stuffer material and return envelope, then sealing a direct-mail package, all in one process. The market for this application is expanding and could enhance the company's long-term growth. We believe Scanforms is the only public company working exclusively in this field. Scanforms thereby offers the investor a pure play. Investor recognition of the company has not yet begun in earnest. The stock trades at about 2. There are approximately 750,000 shares in the active float.

INTEK Diversified Corp. ($2⁷⁄₁₆: OTC–IDCC) The electronics industry, already a mainstay of U.S. technology, continues to grow in importance and is in the forefront of the now so-called Second Industrial Revolution. Industries such as aerospace and defense, computers, robotics and factory automation, medical technology, communications, and transportation are being transformed through new electronic applications.

forefront

Static electricity can destroy or cause degradation of integrated circuits, resulting in significant downtime and increased maintenance. INTEK is believed to be the only independent, publicly traded company in which the fast-growing electrostatic-discharge-control industry represents a major contribution to revenues and profits. The company has proprietary injection-molding techniques combined with proprietary coating technology.

INTEK has introduced, through its subsidiary Olympic Plastics Company, a line of antistatic packaging and materials handling products designed for manufacturers of electronic integrated circuits. A large percentage of this line is produced by proprietary molds developed and owned by the company. Traditionally, INTEK has served the aerospace and defense industries and developed its antistatic technology to serve the needs of their established customers.

The company's antistatic products include tote boxes, stack bin cups, knitting trays, and polyvials, all made of plastic.

Impetus for the development of an electrostatic-discharge-control market has been given by Department of Defense emphasis on quality, as well as by commercial enterprises realizing the costs of equipment failure. As technology has become more pervasive, this highly-fragmented industry has grown with it.

Growth is anticipated through increased market penetration, expanded geographic marketing as well as acquisitions. During the second quarter of 1984, INTEK acquired Bengal, Inc., a leading supplier of antistatic resin. With the acquisition of Bengal, INTEK is believed to be the only plastic injection molding company with antistatic coating technology. Bengal has a broad base of compounds and has a patented compound for one of only two coatings approved by the military. In January 1984, INTEK also purchased Quick Serve Plastic, Inc. In early 1985, INTEK negotiated with IMSC Corp., which has the only automated system to test the static sensitivity of individual components. This high-tech company will add more vertical integration and will give INTEK more of a technology image, as well. The traditional product line produces very-close-tolerance molded plastic parts meeting stringent NASA, FAA, and military specifications. Sales of this line are to military-oriented companies and to Fortune 500 clientele. INTEK holds promise of becoming a leader in the fast-growing electrostatic-discharge-control industry and holds significant investment merit. The current acquisition negotiations with IMCS could immediately expand INTEK's IMCS could immediately expand INTEK's horizons.

At the 1984 year-end INTEK had about $1 million in cash and a 1.6 to 1 current ratio. Long-term debt comprised about 12 percent of stockholders' equity. Sales in

1984 increased to $8.6 million from $4.8 the year before. Earnings per share reached 25¢ from 15¢ last year.

The stock trades around 2⅞. There are 9 million shares authorized of which 3.2 million are outstanding. The float of INTEK is approximately 1.9 million shares.

General Employment Enterprises ($3: ASE–JOB)

General Employment is an established, innovative, and rapidly growing operator of employment agencies. Through fifty offices located in thirty states, the company places salaried personnel in engineering, data processing, technical, administrative, clerical, and security positions. Each office is managed by a company employee and provided with various services. The company's income is derived from placement fees.

Between 1976 and 1981 General Employment experienced exceptional growth, with profits soaring from 1¢ a share to 87¢ a share. This trend ended abruptly in 1982 when the severe recession led to a sharp slowdown in employment growth and a deficit. In 1982 the company scaled back its operations considerably in the face of recession-reduced demand for its services.

During 1983 the company began a national advertising campaign and established special employer service contracts whereby companies list all their job openings with General in return for a lower fee (preferred client agreement). It also began a networking system through which its different placement agencies exchange job applicants and jobs. Operations returned to profitable levels in the first quarter of the fiscal year ending September 30, 1983.

Presently, its agencies are much more heavily concentrated in the Sun Belt areas. Expenses have been reduced, margins have been steadily improving, and several innovations also appear to be paying off. During the March 1985 quarter, a slow one for the economy in general, profits gained 20 percent. Estimates run at 40¢ a share for fiscal 1985 (ending September 30) versus 1984 results of 33¢ a share. Revenues are projected at $15 million or more, and long-term growth of 20 percent appears obtainable.

There are 1,447,401 common shares outstanding of which officers and directors own some 34 percent. Shareholders of record total 1,665. With the exception of a modest capitalization of leases, there is virtually no long-term debt. A current cash yield of 20¢ returns an approximate 5 percent at today's market. As a low-priced special situations candidate, General Employment is deserving of attention.

AW Computer Systems, Inc. ($3½: OTC–AWCSA) An outstanding value at the $2 Window is a small company with an exciting future, AW Computer Systems, Inc., located in southern New Jersey. Briefly, AW Computer designs, develops and markets on-line, real-time integrated point-of-scale systems to the retailing industry. The company's products allow NCR cash registers to communicate with IBM Series/1, the most widely used processor, and PC-AT computers utilizing IBM's Systems Network Architecture (SNA). Additionally, AW Computer allows different generations and models of cash registers to operate in one integrated system as well as enhancing the functionality of older cash registers.

IBM mainframe computers have traditionally been widely used as headquarter computers. With the IBM SNA now the standard for linking remote locations to headquarter computers, IBM is expanding its retail capabilities. For those large retailers wishing to enhance their computer operations by utilizing IBM based computer equipment but currently using NCR cash registers, AW Computer has the solution.

Cash registers are expensive, about $4,000 each, and require time-consuming installations. This provides a compelling reason for large retailers to extend the useful life of older cash registers if they can be upgraded. The AW Computer Systems contract with Montgomery Ward was priced at $3.3 million encompassing approximately 300 stores. There is a great dollar savings compared to the cost of replacing cash registers in 300 such stores, estimated to be in the tens of millions of dollars. Just the cost of replacing the cash registers alone in 300 stores would have been approximately $30 million (using our assumption) or almost ten times the cost of the AW Computer system, providing a savings of $26.7 million. Add to this cost savings the communication software, transition expense, installation costs, etc., and the numbers grow to a more significant savings.

For older NCR cash registers, AW Computer will not only link them to more powerful IBM computers but add important functions: price look-up; credit/debt card authorization; check authorization; in store department/class totals; in-store cash audit; electronic mail; etc. These and other functions will provide timely management reports enabling more efficient operations.

In addition to allowing NCR cash registers to communicate with the more powerful IBM computers and enhanced functionality, AW Computer provides for the transition of one model or make of cash register to another. Eventually, cash registers must be replaced and AW Computer will integrate old and new systems to prevent downtime and continuity of operations whether replacing the current machines with new models of the same manufacturer or changing manufacturers.

A small company such as AW Computer could have a difficult time marketing its impressive technology. However, IBM, which sees the retail market as large and important, has designated AW Computer as a Complementary Marketing Organization. This agreement provides for a mutual identification of prospects and specifies each company's responsibilities. In a similar fashion, AW Computer and IBM Canada, Ltd. have signed a marketing assistance agreement. With AW's computer communication capabilities, IBM will be able to penetrate the in-store and headquarter computer markets and provide retailers with more independence from NCR systems. Of course, once IBM has the computer systems in place, they will be able to more effectively compete for the large-dollar cash register contracts.

AW Computer is completing the installation of its systems into 300 Montgomery Ward stores. Mervyn's, a 110-store subsidiary of Dayton-Hudson, is currently being installed, and Eaton's, a 100-store Canadian retailer, has signed a contract and systems will begin to be installed by the end of 1985. Other contracts are expected to be announced in the near future.

Besides communicating between NCR cash registers and the IBM Series/1 computer, which can handle up to 150 cash registers, AW Computer has adapted this technology to utilize an IBM PC-AT for operations which do not utilize over 30 cash registers. There is also a price advantage as the PC-AT is approximately one-third the cost of the Series/1. The capability to handle an increased number of cash registers by PC-AT is expected. For the near future, two PC-ATs could replace the Series/1 and achieve cost savings for the retailer with the added advantage that if one PC-AT went down, the other could run the entire operation at a limited speed in many retail stores. Two PC-AT computers does provide for a back-up, whereas the Series/1 does not.

In addition to increased penetration of retail chains, AW Computer has a bright future from other opportunities. The company is currently exploring adapting its systems to supermarket chains that have many older cash registers that need to be upgraded. AW Computer and Montgomery Ward are currently testing an AW debit card reader with Bank of America's VERSATEL Automated Teller Machines. Further, each customer is required to enter into a maintenance agreement which enhances revenues and increases the cash flow to the company. Software and hardware changes among established customers provide for converting its software systems to a XENIX (IBM's version of Unix) operating system, giving added capabilities to its system. Additionally, the company's application programs are being rewritten in the "C" language, which also enhances the software. Finally, some customers are investigating replacing the Series/1 computers with dual PC-ATs to aid reliability.

The shares of AW Computer Systems offer an unusual combination of values for a stock priced so low. Earnings for the year-end 1985 at this writing offer the prospect of a 40 percent or greater improvement and a like gain in the following year is anticipated. There are currently about 3,200,000 shares outstanding, of which approximately half are traded in the Over-the-Counter marker. Earnings per share are forecast at 18¢ or better for the current year and possibly as high as 30¢ in 1986. All things considered, AW Computer could be one of the most winning $2 Window choices.

Financial News Network, Inc. ($5¼: OTC–FNNI) This is a unique cable television enterprise. It started out offering financial services exclusively but has since added extensive sports coverage.

FNN broadcasts its live business programs and News service five days a week to cable and UHF affiliates across Canada and the U.S. via communication satellite. Programming originates both in Wall Street and in its Santa Monica Studio, and is broadcast live, except for a few cases where it is transmitted by delayed-tape.

The program is divided into four segments: Business Today, Money Talk, Market Watch and Wall Street Final. A key feature is a continuous business and sports information service (8 P.M. to midnight) giving instant summary of the day's key business information and sports results as available.

There is also a weekend program through A. B. Sports (a subsidiary of Anheuser Busch). This does not compete, however, with live sports events.

The FNN signal now reaches 20 million homes and generates revenues from spot 30-second commercials. Average charge is about $500 but this will increase as popularity of the system grows. The aim is to get 20 of these spot commercials an hour. (Present rate is probably below 45% utilization.) Fees are also derived from subscribers but the rate is low (about 1.5 cents per subscriber). Both rates and subscribers should move upward.

After an investment of over $20 million in debt and equity, and three years of growing pains and operating losses, FNN is now in the black and may earn from 30 cents to 40 cents a share on the 10.15 million shares outstanding in the current fiscal year (ending August 31, 1986).

Management has been streamlined, costs controlled and Financial News Network shares appear to have a unique speculative merit. Cable shares that have staked out strategic territory are in demand both by speculators and by possible acquirers. The combination of financial and sports telecasting should be a winning one.

We look for $16 million in revenue in fiscal 1986 and $3.4 million in net income. Share prices should move higher to reflect profitability; in the past, they traded as high as $10 even though the company was losing $5 million a year!

Chapman Energy Inc. ($3¾: OTC–CHPN) Chapman is an ably managed, diversified oil and gas operation noted for its low-cost production. It is headed by former Texas governor and Secretary of Treasury John B. Connally and boasts a skilled management team that can find oil and also identify troubled companies that can be acquired at distress prices.

Since formation in 1982, company assets have grown from $4 million to more than $67 million. In 1984 Chapman grossed $14.5 million and earned $2,374,000, or $111 a share. The company has a 60 percent interest in a 900-mile Kansas pipeline, which provides an outlet for production and excellent cash flow. Management owns about 65 percent of the stock of Chapman.

There are 13,165,000 shares of Chapman outstanding, with average daily trading volume about 20,000 shares.

The efficiency of the company and its growth rate are impressive. Classify this issue in the growth category.

Southern Hospitality Corp. ($4¼: OTC–SHOS) Southern Hospitality is a lower-priced equity representing a leveraged speculation in probably the most efficient chain of Wendy's franchises in the country.

On May 31, 1985, the company had in operation fifty-two units. Of these, thirty-two were Wendy's and twenty were

Mr. Gatti's Pizza units in the fast-growing Sun Belt areas of Nashville and Memphis, Tennessee. Plans involve the expansion of Southern Hospitality to other areas, with sixty-five units in play at the end of the May 31, 1986 fiscal year. In fiscal 1985 capital expenditures were about $5.4 million—$4 million in new construction and $1.4 million in renovations.

There are 4,787,000 shares of Southern Hospitality, which earned 44¢ in 1984. We look for 60¢ or more in 1986. An active trading issue, and some day perhaps a sellout!

Cybermatics Inc. ($1⅞: OTC–CYBR) Cybermatics Inc. is the largest manufacturer of business forms, labels, and label/form combinations on the East coast. Growing and profitable, the stock of this little-known firm trades at an absolutely and relatively low level, a fact which has obscured the investment values of the company. Currently, Cybermatics posts a $2 million market value despite its revenues of over $20 million and $4 million net worth. With a modest price/earnings ratio of 4.5, we believe Cybermatics is capable of further sales and earnings growth, which could lead the market to place a higher price evaluation on the company. Cybermatics is capitalized modestly with approximately 1,339,000 common shares outstanding, of which 53 percent is closely held.

REVIVAL AND SPECIAL SITUATION STOCKS

Pullman Transportation Co., Inc. ($6½: OTC–PULL) Pullman is a new company with growth characteristics. It was launched as a successor to one of the largest builders of railroad cars, The Pullman Company, which used to make Pullman sleeping cars (and other rolling stock) and lease them to American railways. On January 1, 1984, the freight car assets of the company were sold to Trinity Industries for approximately $17.3 million, plus a perpetual 2 percent license fee for every freight car Trinity sells from Pullman facilities.

At the same time Pullman acquired substantially all the assets and business of Trailmobile and components of UOP Aircraft for $28 million in cash and stock, setting the stage for a totally restructured enterprise with seven plants and 2,500 employees. Trailmobile primarily manufactures dry vans and refrigerated units, produced in a single plant capable of turning out customized trailers with assembly-line efficiency. Trailmobile is second only to Fruehauf in truck trailers and can produce 15,000 units a year. The division is also the largest distributor of generic parts, a stable business generating 50 percent of its profits. Gross revenues, $179 million in 1984, are projected to reach $230 million in 1985.

UOP Aircraft manufactures commercial aircraft seats and galleys for new aircraft and retrofitting for existing planes. An exciting new development is SINGLE-SERV, a patented food service system combining heating and chilling of meals in one mobile cart. TWA is using SINGL-SERV.

REDM Industries, a maker of electric and electronic components, was acquired October 1, 1984, generating revenues of about $40 million. REDM, with four divisions, makes connectors at Eby Co., custom power supplies at Hyperion Industries, fusing and arming devices for ordinance use at Rexon Technology, and thermoplastic molds at Techniplast Inc. About 25 percent of REDM revenues is military and 75 percent commercial.

Pullman benefits from an able and seasoned management coming from Wheelabrator-Frye, a very successful company now part of Signal. It is a lively company with an interesting product diversity. It should gross $325 million in fiscal 1985 and earn above 50¢ a share. Ahead lies a capability for rapid growth both internally and by more acquisitions.   *I 6*

There are 21 million common shares outstanding plus warrants to buy 1.5 million shares at 4 until February 24, 1988. The stock trades at 6⅞ and the warrant at 6¾.

In July 1985 there was a proposal to merge Pullman with Peabody International. The proposal was approved by both company boards. The combined company is Pullman-Peabody International, with its shares listed on NYSE.

Wilshire Oil Company of Texas ($6¼: NYSE–WOC) Wilshire was selected on the basis of its remarkable showing in 1984. Revenues for the year were $17,151,000, up 61 percent from the $10.6 million reported a year earlier. Net income was 45¢ a share contrasted with 26¢ a year earlier. The chairman, Nathan White, stated that, "To achieve these results in today's weak oil market makes Wilshire stand out as a top performer in the industry."

We expect this forward motion to continue in 1985–1986 and believe Wilshire common, trading at 6½ on the NYSE, will continue to perform well. Since 1980, the price of oil has declined 25 percent, but the cost of production has lowered by about 50 percent. This development is favorable to efficient producers such as Wilshire. There are 8,263,000 shares of common outstanding.

The Hallwood Group, Inc. ($1⅛: NYSE–HWG)   It is unusual to find a stock, listed on NYSE, selling below $2 and paying a dividend! Such an issue is Hallwood, and we regard it as a speculation of unique promise. Hallwood Group was created April 30, 1984, as a merger of Atlantic Metropolitan Corp. and Umet properties. The major corporate objective is the rescue of financially distressed companies by restructuring their debt and restoring their earning power.

Hallwood operates under two divisions: investment banking and real estate. The investment banking division is run in conjunction with a 47.5 percent ownership of Interallianz Hallwood, an institution organized in 1983 by Hallwood and Interallianz (a Swiss bank owned by several prestigious institutions, including Winterthur, the foremost Swiss insurance company, Nippon Credit Bank, Bank Leu, Toshiba, and Toyota).

After Hallwood has identified a troubled company as a suitable candidate, it negotiates reduction or retirement of debt and the infusion of new capital by a rights offering. Hallwood thus winds up with a substantial share of ownership and control of the revived company. In a recent reorganization of Saxon Oil, Hallwood received 2 million shares of new Saxon stock as a fee and subscribed to 1.9 million shares at 85¢, winding up with 3.9 million shares of common plus cash fees of $1.8 million payable over five years.

The company's real estate sector includes ownership, operation, management, and sale of commercial and residential properties in the United States and the United Kingdom. About 54 percent of investments are in shopping centers in California, Michigan, and Illinois.

Atlantic and Umet, before the merger, were REITS with combined operating properties valued (July 31, 1984) at $68.9 million. Hallwood is now capitalized by $25.6 million in long-term debt and 33.4 million shares of common stock. There is also an issue of 4,391,000 $8 par preferred, convertible into seven shares of common. Both issues are listed on the NYSE. Indicated 1985 earnings were 30¢ a share.

Hallwood is an unusual company poised to rescue, and profit from, troubled companies. Hallwood had identified, in early 1985, some 400 companies meeting its criteria of virtual bankruptcy and urgent need of financial guidance and assistance. HWG shares may represent a $2 Window of opportunity.

TRADING RANGE STOCKS

The Volatile Airline Industry   An excellent arena for trading-range speculation is the airline industry. It is notably cyclical, following a quite regular pattern of ups and downs over the last decade, making possible recurrent trading gains of 50 percent in active stocks. Airline shares are, indeed, ideal vehicles for those who lean heavily on technical charts for reaching market decisions. According to the conventional wisdom, you should buy airline shares in the teeth of a recession and sell them while the economy is recovering. But don't wait for the crest!

To illustrate, in January 1981 you could have bought American Airlines (AMR) by the bale at $9 a share. From there the airline advanced slowly, picking up momentum in July 1982 (AMR then sold at 14⅝). From then through October 1983 the Standard & Poor's 500 stock index advanced by 45.6 percent. But airline issues had gained 123 percent in this period and peaked in August. They then dipped for a few months, influenced in part by the threat of a price war. This price war didn't take place, and air shares bounced back 30 percent by the end of 1983. Plenty of volatility and scoring opportunities for the nimble trader.

Possibly no other industry is more "group-minded" than airlines. The weak go up with the strong and vice versa, and usually the only mavericks are those skirting bankruptcy or under acute regulatory surveillance. Look at the trading pattern and you will appreciate the almost rhythmic undulation of shares in this industry. Chart reading will clue you in on the current stage in the market cycle, and follow particularly trends in daily volume. No group is more sensitive to upticks on rising volume. When you note these for several days, it is a strong and fairly dependable buy signal.

While there is a pendulum-like action in this group, there are also significant fundamental factors to be tracked:

1. imminence or absence of a fare war;
2. introduction of faster and more economical planes;
3. improvement in traffic growth;
4. new competition (stimulated by industry deregulation);
5. anticipated price changes in aviation fuel;
6. possible mergers;
7. lines troubled by financial or labor problems;
8. lines with inadequate maintenance (and consequently accident-prone); nobody wants to ride, or invest in, an unsafe airline!

With the above considerations in mind, the view of the industry in 1985–1986 is a fairly confident one. Traffic is increasing, fares fairly well stabilized, prospects are for lower crude prices (very important to generating profits), excellent earnings by the leaders (Delta, American, UAL, and Northwest), and compatibility rather than competition developing between the regionals and the trunk carriers.

Several local and regionals have arranged to become feeders of traffic to larger carriers at their network terminals.

Further financial difficulties in the industry are on hold. Pan Am and Eastern, earlier impacted by labor costs, seem to be working out of their problems. The return of Braniff to profitability surprised many an analyst.

Regional carriers report good traffic growth. AMTRAK nearly closed down in 1985. If it does expire later on, more traffic would be diverted to air.

Among the lower-priced issues, which this book features, the airlines on our list would include Pan Am (7⅞), Eastern (7), Republic (9¾), Western (7½), Ozark (14½), Mid-Pacific (3), and Empire (14). This is a general shopping list for low fliers. Get latest reports on the ones that interest you and look at or borrow from a broker charts on those trading most actively. Most are listed on the NYSE or AMEX, which assures action and volume. In general, if an airline stock is trading at its two-year high, you'd better defer purchase. The biggest reason to buy quite indiscriminately would be a sharp drop in the world oil price.

Some people like to keep their profits in the industry that produced them. We know one investor who made a lot of money trading in Eastern and Pan Am. Every time he took a profit, however, he put the money into Delta (probably the best) and now has 1,000 shares—now 43. A good way to fly!

If you keep in mind that air shares are cyclical trading vehicles, then you may structure a program aiming for 50 percent gains within fifteen months. You may reach your target sooner or you may get a "bird" that just never gets off the ground. The idea is to be right two times out of three!

For sporting aviators we have chosen three stocks with active markets, large share capitalizations, and a history of market savings that have created swift trading gains. Because, however, the text of this book was prepared months before you will read it, you must revalue these suggestions in light of changed economic conditions, or have your broker provide late data on other stocks with better flight patterns.

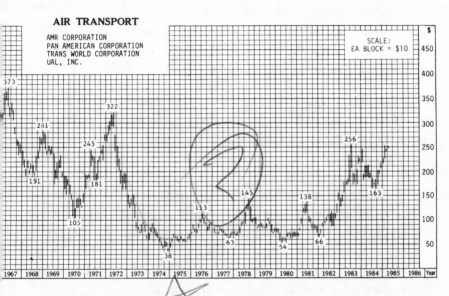

AIR TRANSPORT

AMR CORPORATION
PAN AMERICAN CORPORATION
TRANS WORLD CORPORATION
UAL, INC.

SCALE:
EA BLOCK = $10

PAN AM CORPORATION In the years from 1975 through 1984, Pan Am has ranged in trading between a low of 2 and a high of 10¾, and the average variation between the low and high in any year has been about 150 percent. This almost rhythmic volatility has provided many opportunities for well-timed trading round trips and should continue to do so in the future. The company always seems to remain on the edge of profitability, and the times when it has flirted with bankruptcy have flashed unique buying opportunities. We feel that the line is so large and so essential an international carrier that it will never go out of business; yet by overexpansion, high labor costs, and unprofitable routes in bygone days, it never will deliver an earnings statement or balance sheet to compare with Delta or United.

The stock traded is in Pan Am Corporation, holding company for Pan American World Airways, with major routes to Europe, the Near or Middle East, Egypt, and Latin America, and Pacific routes connecting the United States with Hawaii, the Philippines, Japan, and Australia. In mid-1984 the fleet consisted of forty-three B-747s, sixteen 737s, forty-seven 727s, twelve L-1011s, and one DC-10.

There's plenty of stock for trading: 102.2 million shares, preceded by $1,157 billion in long-term debt including debentures convertible into 29.5 million shares of common. There's also a warrant issue to buy 10 million shares of common at 8 to May 1, 1993. This warrant is a fascinating and leveraged speculation. The stock, as this was written, is trading at 7½, and the warrant at 3⅛. Historically the stock was a buy at 4 and a sell at 8 for formula traders.

Since this was written Pan Am has arranged to sell its Pacific operations to United; and Resorts International was reported as a substantial stockholder in Pan Am.

EASTERN AIRLINES   Eastern, like Pan Am, has had trouble making a profit, and struggling under the heaviest debt load of any major in the business. It, too, has presented an undulating trading market over the past decade with a series of phases where you could buy at 5 and sell at 10 within fifteen months. Thus, for avid traders, and especially chart aficionados, the shares are challenging and potentially rewarding.

Eastern is the second largest airline in the United States in terms of total passengers carried. It serves most major cities on the east coast of North America with routes to the Sunbelt states, California, and the Pacific Northwest. It also has routes to Bermuda, Central and South America, and the Caribbean. It's a huge company, grossing $4 billion a year. Earnings in the past five years have been negligible, and the company has survived by labor concessions from employees, stretched-out debt payments, and employees buying preferred stock (carrying 25 percent of the voting power). We don't think it will go belly up. Historic trading patterns indicate that you can buy at between 4 and 5 and get 9 or 10 a few months later, if your timing is good and you are patient. There's plenty of stock available, 41.3 million shares plus securities convertible into 6.2 million additional shares and warrants to purchase 12.2 million shares.

WESTERN AIRLINES Continuing deficits over the five-year period from 1980 through 1984 have weakened the position of Western Airlines and kept the shares in a low trading range. From 1974 to 1984 the high was 14⅝ (1978) and the low 3⅜ (1982). The line, however, has economic validity and survivor characteristics, and the shares have been a gainful purchase on repeated occasions when they traded below 6.

While still a marginal operation when viewed from its balance sheet, Western should definitely move forward from the deficit of $1.60 a share reported in 1984. Labor conditions have been stabilized under an arrangement where employees accepted 32 percent of the stock in exchange for wage concessions.

The line was restructured with Salt Lake City established as the hub of operations. Routes connect with most West Coast cities, north and south between San Diego and Vancouver, and north to Alaska. International routes connect Los Angeles and San Francisco to Mexico and Hawaii.

Capitalization is leveraged with $426 million in long-term debt, two series of preferred stock (convertible into 5.7 million common shares), and 24 million shares of common—also, warrants to purchase 10,528,000 shares of Western at 9½.

The common sells at 1, the warrant at 1½. The potentials for gain here are improved operating efficiency, a new fleet of Boeing 737s on order, lower fuel costs, and takeover possibilities. Another excellent trading-range stock with timing of purchase assisted by chart reading.

OTHER VALUES

Golden Nugget ($2: NYSE–GNG)   Golden Nugget warrants should perform well in the months ahead. Golden Nugget warrants permit you to buy one share of Golden Nugget common (listed on the NYSE) at 18 until July 1, 1988. The related stock sells today at 10, only 7¾ away from the striking prices and with over three years to run.

Golden Nugget is a lively company—the best of the casino stocks in point of management. GNG owns and operates two casinos: one on the boardwalk at Atlantic City, and the other in downtown Las Vegas. The company has been notably profitable, and the stock was split 5 for 1 in 1983. There are now 35 million common shares and 15 million warrants outstanding.

The company should earn 40¢ a share in 1985 and higher in 1986. Golden Nugget has been aggressive in expansion and in May 1985 made an unsuccessful bid for the new Hilton Hotel in Atlantic City. Casino shares have suffered because some companies have been accused of gangster ownership. Those situations have been cleaned up, and now casino shares are sought for their cash flow and growth.

Gaming shares have a lot of volatility and provide a high beta. These Golden Nugget warrants should prove winners in range trading. Buy them around 2 and sell above 7.

STOCKS IN TODAY'S MARKET

We are now ready to submit a shopping list of stocks illustrative of values in today's market, not as recommendations but as examples. They are a random sampling of low-priced securities available (1) Over-the-Counter, (2) on the American Stock Exchange, and (3) on the New York Stock Exchange.

Over-the-Counter

NAME	PRICE	NAME	PRICE
Aequitron Medical	3⅜	INTEK Diversified	2⁷⁄₁₆
Austron	4⅜	Microsemi	5½
Automated Med. Labs	4⅜	National Bank of Australia	5
AW Computer Systems	3½	Nationwide Legal Services	2⅜
Boonton Electronics	4¼	Nationwide Power	2⁹⁄₁₆
Buffton	5	Northern Air Freight	4¾
Cutco Industries	3⅜	PLM Financial Services	7½
Cybermatics	1⅞	Pullman	6⅞
Datasouth Computer	2⅝	RSI	2¼
Dual Lite	5⅛	Rustenburg Mines	7½
EMF	3	Scanforms	2½
Environdyne Industries	5½	Southern Hospitality	4¼
General Devices	1⅝	Tidbit Alley	3¾
Intech	3⅝	U.S.A. Cafes	5⅛

NOTE: This is a low-priced list of OTC stocks selected at random from the market of September 30, 1985.

Now follows a series of low-priced companies listed on the American and New York stock exchanges.

American Stock Exchange

NAME	PRICE	NAME	PRICE
ADI Electronics	4½	Cosmopolitan Care	2¾
AM International	4⅛	Courtaulds	2⅛
Acme Precision Products	2⅛	DWG	1¾
Acton	1⅛	Damson Oil	3½
Adams Res. & Energy	3¼	Dataram	5⅞
Aeronca	4	De Rose Industries	2½
American Fructose A	5⅜	Delmed	1⅝
American Fructose B	4⅞	Designatronics	4½
Amer. Healthcare Maint.	4	Digicon	1½
American Med. Bldgs.	4⅝	Diodes	3
American Oil & Gas	4¼	Dome Petroleum	1¹⁵/₁₆
American Sci. & Engng.	4⅝	Eagle Clothes	2¼
Ampal American Israel	2	Elsinore	3
Anderson Jacobson	2⅜	Empire of Caroline	5⅞
Argo Petroleum	3¾		
Armatron International	4⅜	Fotomat	1¾
Astrotech International	1⅜	Galaxy Oil	1½
Audiotronics	2½	GEMCO National	2⅜
B.A.T. Industries	3¾	General Employment	3
BRT Realty Trust	2⅝	Genisco Technology	4¾
BSD	3	Global Natural Resources	4
Barco of California	3⅝	Golden West Homes	3
Barnes Engineering	3⅜	Halmi (Robert)	2⅛
Barry (R.G.)	4⅜	Harvey Group	1¼
Bowmar Instruments	4½	Heldor Industries	2½
Buckhorn	3⅛	Hershey Oil	4¼
CMX	1⅜	Hinderliter Industries	2⅛
Campanelli Industries	1¼	Hofmann Industries	2⅝
Cardillo Travel Systems	2⅜	Houston Oil Trust	4¾
CasaBlanca Industries	2½	ICO, Inc.	1⅝
Champion Home Builders	1¾	Imperial Group	2⅞
Cognitronics	4¼	IPM Technology	2⅞

NAME	PRICE	NAME	PRICE
Instrument Systems	1¾	Philippine Long Distance	2
International Banknote	3⅜	Plymouth Rubber B	3⅛
International Proteins	3¼	Pico Products	2⅛
Internatl Thoroughbreds	4½	Pioneer Systems	3⅜
Jet American Air	4⅛	Pope, Evans and Robbins	3¾
Johnson Products	3	Presidio Oil	3½
Jumping-Jacks Shoes	2¾	Punta Gorda Isles	4⅜
Kapok	3⅞	RMS Electronics	3½
Key Co. A	3	Redlaw Industries	2⅝
Key Co. B	3⅜	Rex-Noreco	3⅞
Kinark	3⅜	Rooney, Pace Group	2
Kirby Exploration	2⅝	SMD Industries	3¼
Kit Manufacturing	4⅞	San Carlos Milling	1
Kleer-Vu Industries	2⅛	Sanmark-Stardust Inc.	4¾
LSB Industries	2	Sceptre Resources	3⅝
LaBarge	1¾	Science Management	5⅝
Lifestyle Restaurants	1¾	Seaport	1⅝
Lodge & Shipley	1⅝	Seis Pros	2
		Selas	4⅞
MCO Resources	1¼	Semtech	3¼
MSR Exploration	2½	SIFCO Industries	5
Marathon Office Supply	3⅜	Silvercrest Industries	4
McDowell Enterprises	5¾	Simco Stores	3⅛
McRae Industries B	3⅞	Sterling Electronics	2
Michigan General	4	Struther Wells	2
Mortronics	1½	Summit Energy	4¾
Newberry Energy	3¾	Superior Care	1
Noel Industries	2¾	Susquehanna Corp.	4
Nolex	2⅝	Swift Energy	1⅝
Nu Horizons Elec.	3¼	Tie/Communications	4⅜
Nuclear Data	5	TechAmerica Group	3
Odetics A	4⅞	Technical Tape	3⅞
O'okiep Copper	4¾	Techodyne	1½
Oriole Homes A	4½	TeleConcepts	1⅞
Oriole Homes B	4½	Telesphere International	4
Pay-Fone Systems	4⅛	Texas American Energy	4¾
Petro-Lewis	2¾	Texscan	1

NAME	PRICE	NAME	PRICE
Torotel	3⅛	Weatherford International	3⅜
Total Petroleum Warrants	2	Wedco Technology	3¼
Tubos de Acaro de Mexico	2¾	Wells-Gardner Electronics	2¾
United Foods A	1⅝	Wespercorp	1⅜
United Foods B	1½	Wichita Industries	2¾
Vermont Research	3¾	Wolf (Howard B.)	2¾
Vertipile	4	Worldwide Energy	3⅞
Viatech	6	Zimmer	4⅛
Vicon Industries	4⅝		

New York Stock Exchange

NAME	PRICE	NAME	PRICE
Allis-Chalmers	4¼	Oak Industries	2
Anacomp	3	Parker Drilling	4⅜
Bank of Texas	2⅛	Pan American warrants	3⅛
British Land	4⅛	Prudential Realty	2
Buttes	1⅜	Publicker	2⅞
Consumers Power	7	Ronson	2⅛
Electronic Assoc.	4	Texas International	3⅝
First Pennsylvania Bank	6	Texfi	2¾
Galveston-Houston	3⅜	Tosco	3¾
Gruntal	6¼	United Park City Mines	3
Management Assistance	3⅛	Varco	4¾
Massey-Ferguson	2⅝	Western Air warrants	2⅝
MESTEK	3½	World Air	3⅜
Northgate	3	Wurlitzer	3⅛

The above securities were selected from the market of October 23, 1985. They are presented in no sense as recommendations but merely to indicate the range and diversity of equities available. Before making any investment decisions on these or any other securities mentioned in this book, get the latest available information and quotations and assure yourself about the speculative potentials (or absence thereof) in each case.

7

The Art of Timely Selling and Successful Profit Taking

In the earlier chapters we covered the opportunities existing in Wall Street's bargain basement, cited winning low-priced stocks of the past, and prepared a representative shopping list of $2 stocks now available. Further, a selection of $2 Window candidates was presented. These lists and selections are for purposes of illustration, and the shares mentioned, or described in capsule, may have changed in price and in their potential for gain (if any), by the time you get to read this book.

Before making any decision to buy or sell, however, you should get the latest information possible about the issue that interests you (get a quarterly or annual report, at the least), and, most important, you should note the trend of earnings, expectation of dividends or dividend increases, and any possibility that may exist for takeover of the company. Watch also the market action of the stock for a few days before you make a decision. Generally, if a stock is on an "uptick," that is, selling higher at the close of a day than a day earlier, and if volume is increasing, the stock may be under accumulation. You will then be buying into a strong market. Indeed, your best purchases may be made when you buy a stock as volume of trading in it and price quotations are rising.

Similarly, if you consider selling, your decision may be confirmed by the appearance of increasing volume on the down side. If the issue has crested, it is important that you sell it early.

Strategy and Timing   All the hundreds of books and thousands of articles on Wall Street, and the dozens of current investment services have been designed to guide you in three major areas: (1) what to buy; (2) when to buy; (3) when to sell. In reviewing much of this literature, we have observed that many of these books, articles, and market studies provide excellent and diverse counsel in the first two sectors, but are deficient in the third. Frankly, we know of no well-organized source of defined materials, procedures, or formulas that have provided consistently dependable and effective decision making counsel on when to sell stocks and pin down your profits.

Accordingly we have interviewed some of the most successful traders and investment professionals to get their viewpoints and observe their strategies in handling investment portfolios of all sizes. We have gathered and winnowed the adages and axioms of the Street on when to cash in and have researched a group of useful ratios and indices that monitor the altitude of markets. We have referred to recognized experts in both fundamental and technical analysis.

As a result, we believe we have assembled some extremely useful ideas on maximizing your profit retention. We think the data we have organized should be continuously useful to you and may make a significant contribution to your future success in stock trading. Historically, most individuals have been too reluctant to sell and might benefit from the philosophy of the famously rich Baron Rothschild who contended that he "always sold too soon!"

It should be observed at the outset that the decision to sell is an individual one reached most often by a blending of emotion and logic. In general, people sell stocks because (1) they need money to buy a house, reduce a mortgage, or send a child to college; (2) they sense that the market is too high; (3) they are itchy to cash in on a profit before it fades; (4) they have lost faith in a specific stock; (5) they want to switch to a more promising or livelier issue; (6) they received a margin call; or (7) they are in fright or panic. Added to these traditional reasons for selling, we aim to develop, as we go along, logical reasons for a general liquidation or exiting from particular stocks.

In deciding whether or not to sell, a major consideration should be the level of the whole market. Has a speculative boom sent a majority of stocks to prices that are absurd and at unreal levels?

In this chapter, we shall consider a spectrum of marketable securities with a view to gleaning from the past those conditions which made an entire market a sale. We shall look to that level of trading which exploded to great heights, fueled by euphoria, enthusiasm, peak corporate profits, prosperity, and speculative zeal, which in turn motivated hundreds of thousands of new players to buy stocks.

Expansion and Depression As you look over the Dow Jones Industrial Average (DJIA) chart for the past fifty-six years (on the following page), you will note two stand-out periods when the market peaked and it was time to sell. These zeniths were in 1929 and 1972; but there were several cyclical tops in between where prudence should have called for substantial selling.

The classic peak was in autumn 1929, just before the onset of the Great Depression. We are not going to write a history of the period in-depth, but we do want to accent those forces that propelled stocks to historic highs so that we may recognize similar or parallel conditions in the future and sell before a deluge.

In the early 1920s, there was a quick depression followed by a period of steadily expanding prosperity. The motor car industry exploded, bringing with it high profitability to related makers of auto parts and tires, to makers of cement for highways, and to giant oil companies who supplied the gas and lubrication. Railways reached their zenith before cars, buses, and later the airlines came in and all but destroyed the rails' passenger business. The great companies of the era were Standard Oil of New Jersey, New York Central, Woolworth, U.S. Steel, General Motors, General Electric, National City Bank, Coca-Cola, and Consolidated Edison. The utility holding companies evolved, such as Middle West Utilities, American Gas and Electric, American Power and Light, and North American Company. Also, investment trusts (Goldman Sachs, Shenandoah, American Founders) and the technology stock of the era (Radio Corp.) were developed. Finally, there was the then maximum swindle, Kreuger & Toll.

The stock market, buoyed by persistent annual gains in corporate profits and dividends, no inflation, low interest rates (savings banks paid 4 percent), installment purchase of motor cars, and only 10 percent margins on stock purchases moved steadily upward from 1926 to September 1929. By 1929, there were 1.5 million Americans in the market, not for safety or income, but simply to make killings! The percentage of individuals' total assets represented by margin loans was unreal, with devastating down-

THE STOCK PICTURE

DOW-JONES INDUSTRIAL AVERAGE

Stocks Included in This Average.

ALLIED CORPORATION
ALCOA CORPORATION
AMERICAN BRANDS, INC.
AMERICAN CAN COMPANY
AMERICAN EXPRESS CO.
AMERICAN T. & T. CO.
BETHLEHEM STEEL CORPORATION
CHEVRON CORPORATION
DUPONT (E.I.) DE NEMOURS & CO.
EASTMAN KODAK COMPANY
EXXON CORPORATION
GENERAL ELECTRIC COMPANY
GENERAL FOODS CORPORATION
GENERAL MOTORS CORPORATION
GOODYEAR TIRE & RUBBER CO.
LTD.
INTERNATIONAL BUSINESS MACHINES
INTERNATIONAL HARVESTER CO,
INTERNATIONAL PAPER COMPANY
MERCK & COMPANY
MINNESOTA MINING & MFG. CO.
OWENS ILLINOIS, INC.
PROCTER & GAMBLE COMPANY
SEARS, ROEBUCK & COMPANY
TEXACO, INC.
UNION CARBIDE CORPORATION
UNITED STATES STEEL CORPORATION
UNITED TECHNOLOGIES CORPORATION
WESTINGHOUSE ELECTRIC CORP,
WOOLWORTH (F.W.) COMPANY

MAY
1985
* *

M. C. HORSEY & COMPANY, Publishers
120 SOUTH BLVD.
SALISBURY, MARYLAND 21801

1927–1963

Yr. 19 '27 '28 '29 '30 '31 '32 '33 '34 '35 '36 '37 '38 '39 '40 '41 '42 '43 '44 '45 '46 '47 '48 '49 '50 '51 '52 '53 '54 '55 '56 '57 '58 '59 '60 '61 '62 '63

1625 1500 1375 1250 1125 1000 875 750 625 500 375 250 125

386 41 196 213 254 524 416 564 688 741 525

3

THE STOCK PICTURE

QUOT RON
INDU

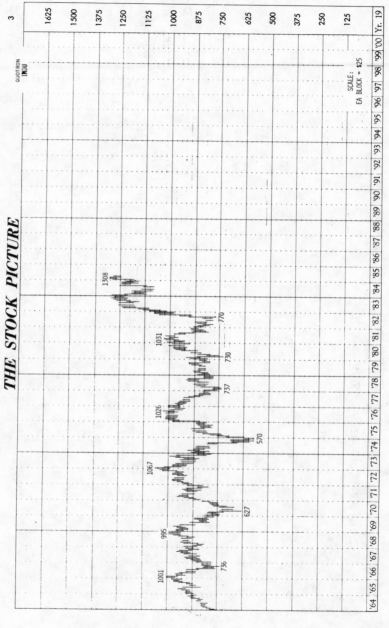

1964–1985

SCALE:
EA BLOCK = $25

| 1625 | 1500 | 1375 | 1250 | 1125 | 1000 | 875 | 750 | 625 | 500 | 375 | 250 | 125 | Yr. 19 |

'64 '65 '66 '67 '68 '69 '70 '71 '72 '73 '74 '75 '76 '77 '78 '79 '80 '81 '82 '83 '84 '85 '86 '87 '88 '89 '90 '91 '92 '93 '94 '95 '96 '97 '98 '99 '00

1308

1031

1026

1067

1001

995

756

627

570

737

750

770

side destructive leverage. A schoolteacher making $5,000 a year might have had $7,500 in margin loans on stocks. In 1928 and 1929, stocks often recorded instant gains. Radio Corp. (which reached a high of over 400) would gain fifteen or twenty points in a single day!

Conditions began to explode in 1927. The first five million shares a day traded on the New York Stock Exchange was June 12, 1928. The market was fueled by call money, that is, funds loaned to stock exchange firms for reloan to their stock buyers on margins. It was not just the banks that loaned these funds, but also large corporations. It seemed to be sound lending. With marketable stocks as collateral, attractive interest rates ranged from 6 percent to 20 percent at the high point. Stocks crested in 1929. Indeed, a key to the excesses of the era was the rapid volume expansion of call money. Call loans were $3.5 billion at the 1927 year-end, $4 billion by June 1928, and $7 billion by August 1929.

In any event, stocks with interim dips (and a heavy sell-off in December 1928) continued to move up until autumn 1929. The greatest percentage upswing was during 1928 when Radio Corp. moved from 85 to 420, Montgomery Ward from 117 to 440, and Dupont from 309 to 525. It was so easy to make money until October 1929!

In March 1929, there was a sell-off that might have ended the boom, but more call money was made available. In August 1929, the rediscount rate was raised from 5 percent to 6 percent, but this was too little and too late. In September, heavy selling began. On October 24, 1929, 12,900,000 shares were traded (a new record) and bids faded all over the place. At the day's end, thousands of margin calls were sent out. Tuesday, October 29, was doomsday. The market plummeted, and 16,410,030 shares were traded. Westinghouse, which had sold at 280 in September, hit 100, and Goldman Sachs dropped from 60 to 35 during this fatal day. Tens of thousands couldn't answer their margin calls and were "sold out" at progressively lower prices, which in turn created new margin calls for those still hanging on.

This saga of panic need not be prolonged. From 1929 to 1932 the DJIA dipped from a high of 386 (September 1929) to a low of 41 (July 1932), and the Great Depression set in with a vengeance.

Between 1929 and 1932 there were several rallies in the market, which carried stocks back part of the way, but these only served, in the long run, as a smoke screen for the prevailing disaster. The ultimate erosion was fantastic! Look at these quotations:

STOCK	1929 HIGH	1932 LOW
Radio Corp. (after 3-for-1 split)	114¾	2½
Montgomery Ward	156⅞	3½
General Motors	91¾	7⅝
Goldman Sachs	121¼	1
North American Co.	186¾	13¾
Chrysler	135	5
U.S. Steel	261	21¼
New York Central	256½	8¾

This debacle ordained the Great Depression. By the time it was over, 25 percent of the labor force was unemployed, homes and farms were foreclosed by the hundred-thousands, and one-third of railway mileage entered receivership. If ever there had been need for warning signals to stockholders, it was in 1929. Yet some of the signs were there: (1) huge percentage increases in call money fueling continued rises in share prices; (2) stocks selling at unreal high price/earnings ratios, with the DJIA reaching a P/E ratio of 17; (3) a total disdain for income—capital gains were everything; (4) DJIA selling at more than two times book value; (5) unrealistic bidding up of prices—Radio Corp. sold at more than 400 yet never had paid a dividend; Technicolor Corp., a new dimension in movies, sold as high as 100 before diving to 1 in 1932.

There have been many later periods where stocks moved up to levels where sales should have been considered, but the 1972 period seems best indicated on the charts. The DJIA recrossed the 1000 mark and remained on a fairly high plateau for the next six years. The 1972 key signal of a topping-off phase was the popularity of stocks in general. Between 1970 and 1972, McDonald's Corp., Avon Products, and Polaroid Corp. all sold at seventy times earnings or higher, indicating excessive market zeal. Unsatisfactory conditions were further documented by the departure from the gold standard on August 15, 1971, wage and price controls, and the 1972 Watergate scandal. Finally, the 400 percent rise in Arab oil should have told us all that our investment prospects would fade as fuel costs soared.

However, it is much more difficult to define the crest of an economic cycle than the crest in an industry or a dominant company within it. At the crest of 1972, the DJIA recrossed the 1000 mark as it had in 1966, but this again proved to be too high a level to maintain. The sell-off to the 1974 lows put a damper on speculation that was to persist for a decade. Investors by the droves deserted the stock market, which showed little promise, and put their money into bonds, which in 1974 and for most of the time since has yielded 12 to 15 percent.

Yet the signals to sell stocks at the 1972 crest were not easy to discern. The most important clues might have been the departure from the gold standard, wage and price controls, and the rising level of interest rates.

We trust speculative activity will never again reach ruinous extremes, but we do derive some lessons.

1. Sell when the DJIA reaches an excessive level—17 times earnings or twice book values.
2. Sell on any 100 percent increase in margin buying.
3. Sell when the DJIA stock yield goes as low as 3½ percent.
4. Sell when the clamor of the bulls is loudest; if four out of five people you know are buying stocks and raving about particular issues, move out! The market is never that good for any length of time.

From this review of major crests as clues to the timing of sales, we move on to a search for those forces within specific companies that point to prudent and timely selling.

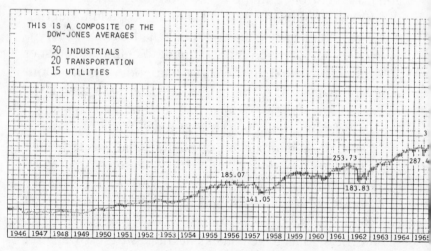

THIS IS A COMPOSITE OF THE DOW-JONES AVERAGES

30 INDUSTRIALS
20 TRANSPORTATION
15 UTILITIES

253.73
287.4
185.07
183.83
141.05

1946 | 1947 | 1948 | 1949 | 1950 | 1951 | 1952 | 1953 | 1954 | 1955 | 1956 | 1957 | 1958 | 1959 | 1960 | 1961 | 1962 | 1963 | 1964 | 1965

THE STOCK PICTURE -- Book of Over 1900 Charts --

FUNDAMENTAL ANALYSIS

Marketable stocks are made to be sold as well as bought. Everyone at some time has a need to convert assets into cash. Stocks have proved useful not only for income and gainful investment of surplus funds, but for the cash values they generate, either through borrowing or by partial or total sale.

The average investor with a portfolio of stocks holds most of them for years, usually income-type equities such as NYNEX, Bankers Trust, American Brands, Consolidated Edison, Pacific Gas & Electric, General Electric, General Motors, and General Foods. Such investors seldom will trade more than 10 percent or 20 percent of their holdings in any year. Trust accounts in banks may trade with a little more frequency. Trusts may turn over their portfolios 30 to

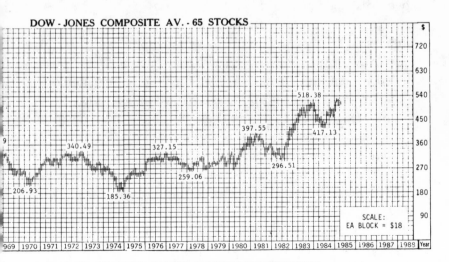

IN DAILY USE BY BANKERS, BROKERS AND INVESTORS EVERYWHERE.

40 percent in a year compared to a 100 percent turnover for aggressive mutual funds.

Individuals who concentrate on trading rather than investing will have a turnover of 50 percent on the average, but they may become victims of an expensive habit—overtrading. A 100 to 200 percent rotation of holdings is excessive; it reduces profits by increasing commissions as a percentage of gain. Don't overtrade! If you're itchy for action, play the horses!

In programming the sale of stocks, to maximize profits, we refer primarily to that section of one's portfolio set aside for trading. For the average investor that would probably mean no more than 20 percent of total holdings in a single year. Most people still hang in there with a solid group of seasoned stocks acquired for income and long-term growth, and they sell these only when earnings or dividends are slipping. As an example, Uniroyal, International Harvester, Inco, Braniff, Asarco, or Caterpillar might have been disposed of in 1981–82.

Nearly everyone with $50,000 or more in the market is interested to some extent in stocks for capital gains. In this context, the securities of preference are actively traded listed issues in a rising stage of earnings and situated in popular industries with impressive growth potentials. Such industries and stocks within them become market favorites attracting enthusiastic sponsorship.

These are the stocks "where the action is" and where perceptive speculators can make killings. When the silver shares were "hot" in 1979, Hecla Mining rose 900 percent and outperformed all other shares on the NYSE! In the late 1940s TV stocks—Admiral, Zenith, RCA, and Motorola—were the sensational performers; in the 1950s life insurance stocks and office equipment—Xerox and IBM—starred; in 1956 and 1958 uranium shares held the spot-

light and made swift fortunes. Then came the phar-
maceuticals; namely, Searle, Pfizer, Upjohn, Merck, and
Syntex. Later in the 1960s savings and loan shares and the
motel equities such as Ramada Inns, Marriott, Holiday
Inns, Travelodge, etc. held the spotlight. Next the hospital
chains, with Humana, American Medicorp, and Hospital
Corp., carried the fashionable labels. During the 1970s the
golds, oils, oil drilling and computer shares were the vir-
tuosi and provided splendid opportunities for gain. In the
early 1980s it was computers and computer related areas,
fast foods, service companies, home health care, and takeover candidates.

All of the industries and the dominant companies
within them went through the four classic market stages,
with strong uptrends along the way. These issues could be
bought and held twelve to twenty-four months and then
sold for handsome capital gains.

These groups moved in random rotation, propelled almost invariably by outstanding increases in earnings; they
gained market recognition and sometimes moved to dramatic highs. Then the trading pace slackened, quotations
faded, and the spotlight moved onto a new group. Such
migration regularly occurs when a given group is driven up
to excessive highs and the prospects for future gains are
dimmed.

These high plateaus are the occasions for liquidation.
However, many hold on stubbornly, miss the peak al-
together, and then berate themselves for not exiting. Good
examples of this descent from highs in 1981 and 1982 were
Union Pacific from 63½ to 31½, Datapoint from 67½ to 11,
Asarco from 47⅞ to 17¼, Standard Oil of Indiana from over
75 to 34⅛, and Dome Petroleum from 21¼ to 4⅛. Each of
these issues was a group favorite and advanced im-
pressively, but successful trading in each depended on

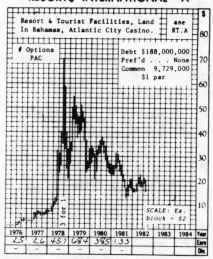

RESORTS INTERNATIONAL "A"

| Resort & Tourist Facilities, Land In Bahamas, Atlantic City Casino. | ase RT.A | $ |

Options PAC

Debt $188,000,000
Pref'd . . . None
Common 9,729,000
$1 par

SCALE: Ea. block = $2

3 for 1

	1976	1977	1978	1979	1980	1981	1982	1983	1984	Year
Earn	.25	.26	4.57	6.84	3.85	1.33				Earn
Div	-	-	-	-	-	-				Div

moving out nimbly near the top. True, the whole market sold off in 1981 and 1982, but all of these declined by a far greater percentage than the Dow Jones Industrial Average.

To illuminate this problem, we have researched these industries: casino stocks (Resorts International) from 1978 to 1979, oil stocks (Standard Oil of Indiana) from 1981 to 1982, and silver stocks (Hecla Mining) from 1979 to 1981. Charts are presented above and on the following page on bellwether issues.

The purpose of a review of the three representative stocks in their group is to illustrate that within the market universe, there are always stocks going up or down in their own orbit, often regardless of, or contrary to, the prevailing and predominant market trend. Rules to "sell the market" have to be modified as popularity and individual share quotations soar or sink in identified groups. Rising earnings and higher dividends may not be enough to continue

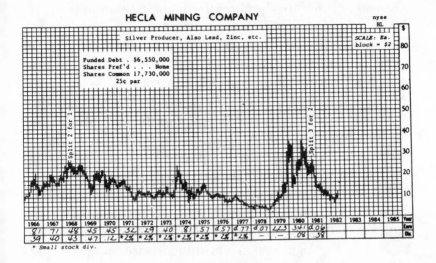

HECLA MINING COMPANY

nyse
HL

Silver Producer, Also Lead, Zinc, etc.

SCALE: Ea.
block = $2

Funded Debt . $6,550,000
Shares Pref'd . . . None
Shares Common 17,730,000
25c par

Split 2 for 1

Split 3 for 2

	1966	1967	1968	1969	1970	1971	1972	1973	1974	1975	1976	1977	1978	1979	1980	1981	1982	1983	1984	1985	Year
Earn	81	71	48	45	45	52	29	40	81	57	d57	d77	d07	223	341	d06					
Div	39	40	43	47	.12	*2%	*2%	*2%	*2%	*2%	*2%	*2%	—	.—	.08	.38					

* Small stock div.

STANDARD OIL CO., INDIANA

nyse
SN

Options
CBOE

Large Midwestern Oil Refiners, Marketers, etc. "AMOCO" Brand.

F'd Debt $3,566,000,000
Shares Pref'd . . . None
Shares Com'n 274,203,000
No par

Shareholders approved new name:
"AMOCO CORPORATION"

Split 2 for 1

Split 2 for 1

SCALE: Ea.
block = $3

	1966	1967	1968	1969	1970	1971	1972	1973	1974	1975	1976	1977	1978	1979	1980	1981	1982	1983	1984	1985	Year
Earn	90	99	109	113	113	123	134	183	338	268	302	352	368	512	654	629	625	639			
Div	.43	.48	.55	.58	.58	.58	60	65	.83	1.00	1.15	1.30	1.40	1.50	2.00	2.60	2.80	2.80	3.00		

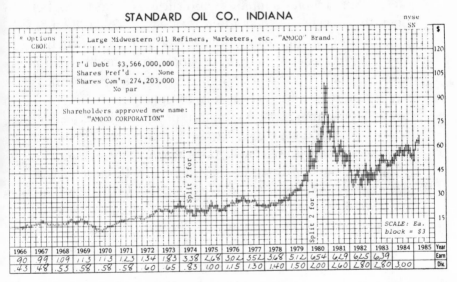

to propel a stock upward after mob psychology and un-
bridled market enthusiasm have already caused an issue to
become visibly overpriced.

How to Sell Before the Crowd   At the $2 Window we are all in favor of the search for stocks that may outperform. But as you consider investing in these or others you believe undervalued, envision a price objective. Remember, the rich Baron Rothschild who "always sold too soon!" Buy stocks before they are popular and sell them when they are!

Decide how high the stock you have carefully researched might reasonably advance within twenty-four months and set a reasonable price objective. Then keep looking for signals along the way that may indicate when the industry and the company in it may be topping out. Look for items in the news that may signal the condition "market overspin." The oil price rises in 1973 and later should have suggested a declining phase in motor car stocks, automobile suppliers, and airlines, due to higher operating costs. The steep interest rates of 1979–1982 indicated that housing elements and building construction were fading sectors, and these stocks were indicated for sale. With such warning, hanging on until a new business cycle restores profitability is a losing play.

Insider selling also is an important signal. This is sometimes noted in the financial press, but there are three services that follow these transactions currently: *The Insiders*, published by the Institute of Economic Research, Fort Lauderdale, Florida; *Consensus of Insiders* (also Fort Lauderdale); and *Insiders Chronicle*, Riverside, Connecticut. Perhaps you can review one of these services at your local broker's office or you may want your own subscription. In any event, for the perceptive, there's a message here. For example, these services noted heavy insider selling in Datapoint for several of the last weeks in 1981. Early in 1982, a sharp decline in profits was reported and the shares declined from a high of 52 to 11, one of the classic instances of the need to sell when the selling is good!

In general, if the P/E ratio of a stock doubles in a year, selling it is a better part of wisdom. Dangerously high multiples are often noted in new issues and early-stage companies.

Growth Stocks   Along these lines, there have developed two popular guidelines for evaluation of growth stocks. The first and more conservative one says that a growth stock doubling its sales and net income within five years can justify a price of 50 percent above the DJIA Price/Earnings multiple. If the current Dow P/E is 10 to 12, then you should pay no more than 15 to 18 times for the growing one.

A second respected formula is that a stock is entitled to sell at its growth rate. To illustrate, if a stock is increasing its net operating income per share at the rate of 35 percent annually, it may properly sell at 35 times earnings and not be regarded as price inflated.

These two approaches result in widely varying appraisals for the same stocks. In practice, the latter formula (a P/E ratio equal to the growth rate) is probably more realistic and will come closer to the market reality. We can state almost categorically that when an authentic growth stock sells at forty times earnings or higher, it is probably overpriced. Such a limit would surely have converted millions of paper profits into cash in the bulging and phasing-out market of 1972 and later on in the early 1980s.

There are certain growth stocks that should never be sold. Among these are the dynamic issues, such as fortune builders for early investors in companies featuring pioneering products, services, and inventions. Of the 40,000 companies whose shares enjoy public trading markets, about 3 percent of them have stocks that should be stubbornly held through thick and thin until their promises are fulfilled. Shares acquired early in Perkin-Elmer, Polaroid, Pfizer,

Control Data, IBM, 3 M, Occidental Petroleum, Schering-Plough, Houston Oil and Minerals, Datapoint, McDonald's Corp., Texas Oil and Gas, Amerada Hess, Tampax, Syntex, Pepsico, all gained more than 3,000 percent within twenty-year periods and selling and/or trading them along the way held the danger of missing the major upswing. But even these super winners had sinking spells that caused many stockholders to panic and sell, thus foreclosing their claims on future market fortunes. If you are in line for a 3,000 percent gain, a modest investment of $10,000 can be fortune building. Dynamic companies increase sales 25 percent a year or more and, typically, pay meager or no cash dividends; many of these issues start out as modest early-phase enterprises in the over-the-counter (OTC) market. They increase in market value by outstanding increases in sales and net profits, by frequent stock dividends, and by a dramatic rise in the P/E multiple at which their shares trade.

But there does come an end to the upcurve of even the greatest performance stocks when their growth rate flattens. For example, Merck, American Home Products, Wang Laboratories, Bally Manufacturing, and Resorts International may no longer be the growth stocks they were. They now move within ranges where they should be sold and replaced when profit taking occasions occur.

Industry Groups For the general run of stocks, we should revert to the DJIA, which is historically a sale at seventeen times earnings. Individual stocks in different industries have their own historic P/E patterns. Steels and metals are sure low P/E ratios; utilities in the middle; and technology, communications, and medical care stocks at the upper levels. P/E ratios for these stocks are shown each day in the Wall Street Journal's NYSE and AMEX stock price tables.

Comparing P/E ratios between industries requires an understanding of the specific industries. What constitutes a high P/E for a steel company may be an abnormally low P/E for a medical care stock. A better barometer for a stock's relative position is to compare its P/E ratio to that of its industry and the DJIA.

We believe that 3 percent of all the stocks in circulation probably should not be sold until their increase in reported sales and profits begin to slack off. If you are nursing along an early-bird eagle, hang on and sell something else if you get itchy or need money. Apart from that, and usually found among the larger mature companies, there are cyclical patterns you should try to identify. Whole industry groups move up and down with pendulum-like regularity; for example, airlines, steels, chemicals, base metals, utilities, building materials, machine tools, consumer products, farm automotive products, and apparel. For those who like activity and partly predictable swings of 30 to 125 percent within eighteen months, the ideas developed in this chapter about active issues may have special utility. In 1981–82, Union Pacific, Cities Service, Louisiana Land and Exploration Co., Asarco, Dome Petroleum, Gulf of Canada, Datapoint, Houston Oil Trust, Freeport-McMoran, Zapata, and Phelps Dodge, all recorded market variations of more than 80 percent. These are seasoned, conservative, and active stocks, not risky penny stocks!

Institutional Investors Many of the companies with large-share capitalizations trading on the NYSE are substantially owned by institutional investors. These seasoned stocks, paying cash dividends, are less likely to decline than most speculative issues. If you look at Standard & Poor's monthly stock guide, you will find a listing of the number of institutions that own a stock and amount of shares totally held—often 20 to 30 percent of the outstanding amount. This type of ownership is an endorsement of the stock's quality and its desirability for income and gain. But these large holders are a sensitive and sheeplike lot. If one decides it's time to sell, several others may quickly follow suit, and often in a matter of weeks, a given stock may shed 20 percent or more of its market value by this progressive selling. By way of example, a recent institutional study indicates that of the worst twenty-five performing S & P stocks in 1981, fourteen were overowned by institutions. Hence, when institutions acquire a large percentage of a company's stock, there may be little additional demand for the stock to push its price higher. It is important that you sell your stocks before they (institutional investors) do!

Generally, these institutional liquidations are motivated by (1) a decline in earnings; (2) an exalted P/E multiple; (3) bad news such as a marketing failure, loss of market percentage, international exchange loss, a misguided merger, increase in debt, or a management fight. General selling of many issues this way may be a signal that the whole market is headed downward.

Since trading on the NYSE is now 70 percent institutional, this action is important for timing purchases or sales. Therefore, it is important to watch in the daily press or in quarterly institutional summaries in *Barron's* the extent of sales by these wholesale investors. Also, look for the block trades of 10,000 shares or more. These trades tell the direction of institutional decisions. If three or four institutions start to sell a stock you own, their selling may become contagious and swiftly depress the price. Of course, pre-

8

Wall Street Folklore

Fundamental analysis, market timing, and technical techniques are not the only indicators. Various observations and studies have been made that are a part of the investment community. We will discuss several popular indicators.

The calendar offers an interesting sequence of market action. For example, the tone of the market is typically set in **January** during the first trading week. The general rule is that if the first week of the New Year and the month of January as a whole are negative, then there is a strong downward bias for the year. This phenomenon appears to be documented by studies conducted which show that the large majority of down years have been preceded by an off market in January. We caution the reader that this is only a seasonal barometer to predict the value of a negative January, and one should exercise caution paying close attention to market conditions that follow, because every down January is not necessarily followed by a down year.

Moving forward, the next most notable event in the calendar is the **April tax-selling period**. Historically, the first half of April outperforms the second half. This is contrary to popular belief—that tax selling causes the stock market to decline during the first few weeks of April and then rebound.

141

July comes with the well-known **summer**, or **mid-year**, **rally**. Here we focus on the Fourth of July. History shows that the Standard & Poor's Composite Index has gained 3 to 4 percent for the five days before the holiday and five days after. The balance of July typically has been a washout, however. The month on the whole has declined almost as many times as it has advanced.

Not to be outdone by Independence Day, **Labor Day** has its own characteristics. During the 1960s and the 1970s, the market indexes during Labor Day weekends declined 60 percent of the time. But, here comes the catch! The decline in September is not believed to be bearish! Rather, it is a reverse barometer. That is, if the market is down during Labor Day week, chances are better for an up market in the following months and vice versa.

Finally, at **year-end during bear markets**, declining stocks sell at very low prices near the conclusion of the calendar year as investors liquidate their holdings for tax purposes. As a general rule, when the S&P Composite Index six-day average for the last four days of December and the first two days of January fails to rise, watch out! It may be a bear, not a bull coming out of the woods.

Cyclical Trading Patterns Cyclical trading patterns among various industries can be identified and success-fully utilized. Typically, aerospace companies are good sales in January; meatpacking, property and liability insurance, railroads, and agricultural machinery companies are sales in February; air-conditioning companies can be sold in March; and machine-tool companies in April.

Trading patterns during the week are also an accepted Wall Street phenomenon. The contrast between the first and last trading day of the week is particularly noteworthy.

Mondays have the highest percentage of down days (about 60 percent). Conversely, Fridays, or the last day of the trading week, close higher about 60 percent of the time. It is noteworthy that only about one out of four Mondays rise after the previous Friday has declined.

The ten-year pattern of stock-market cycles may be difficult to comprehend, but it appears that seventy percent of the time, the third, seventh, and tenth year of the decade are down years. (Most Wall Street folklore has hidden logic to be discovered when examining a phenomenon, but we are totally mystified by this pattern of market behavior.)

Finally, election-trend years are a well-followed indicator of this nature. There is a correlation between presidential elections and stock-market performance. Typically, the market will rise during the year of the election. A Democratic party victory normally spells about a 2 percent decline in the following month compared to about a 3 percent gain with a Republican victory. However, during the entire Republican administrations, the market does not fare as well as it does under Democratic administrations. A recent exception was the Carter term and, of course, the jury is still out on the present Republican administration, which is now in its second term. One last note on election-year market trends is that the market is likely to rise between the end of the last convention and election day more often then not when the incumbent party wins the election.

Pearls of Wisdom   Many a truth is uttered in jest. In the case of selling stocks and in bear markets, gallows humor gives way to rather incisive clichés. We have assembled below some of the more telling quotes from a consortium of Wall Street regulars.

"Sell when the clamor of the bulls is loudest."

"Don't make waves, ride crests."

"Throw away the charts on major bad news."

"The first earnings disappointment won't be the last."

"What comes up very fast comes down just as fast."

"Buy on the rumor; sell on the fact!"

"A breakout [major upswing in stock prices] is almost always followed by a pullback."

"How the market reacts to bad news is much more important than the news."

"Always sell 'too soon.'" *bec if you wait you gonna sell too late.*

"In the stock market nothing recedes like excess."

"Don't hold out for the last eighth."

"In Wall Street a bull makes money, a bear makes money, but a pig, never!"

The reader is cautioned to recognize that Wall Street folklore, seasonal market-trading patterns, and other such phenomena are not necessarily foolproof and reliable predictors. They are, however, widely observed and can at times, over the short term, be significant. Bearing caution in mind, be aware of these peculiarities of the market.

Hemlines Tell Us When to Sell   There exists a long-term relationship between fashion and money. When fashion is mentioned, the immediate reference is to the prevailing style in women's dresses. Actually, fashion is a more generic word. In addition to its traditional application to jeans, bikinis, miniskirts, harem skirts, men's pleated trousers, or plus fours, fashion (the change in mode or style) relates to many facets of life: pop, country and western, or soul music; condominiums; scuba diving; coin and stamp collecting; credit cards; theatrical productions; minicars; ranch houses; supermarkets; and jai-alai. Everybody wants to be in the swing—to outdo and outfashion other people.

Cadillacs beat Chevys, chinchillas beat minks, a brownstone beats a penthouse, and rubies beat diamonds. So it is that women's fashions are a continuing and influential phenomenon; we contend that they will reflect stock prices, and influence market decisions.

Fashion was not really significant until after World War I. Before then, fashion clothes were custom-made, and the dresses sported were not copied widely or converted into mass production. Further, radical changes in style were not widely noticed until the twentieth century. Before 1914, almost all skirts dragged along the floor, while stock prices were of concern to only relatively small numbers of people. However, in the twenties there developed an explosion in both stocks and fashion, as hundreds of thousands more people in the United States could afford both and as volume production of both emerged.

The rationale for the table we have prepared and the whole theory of correlation between stock prices and hemlines originated about 1917. By that time it became apparent that the centers of both fashion and finance were in New York City. Higher incomes placed many thousands of women in a position to dress more modishly, and mass production of women's apparel, developed in New York's garment district, led to nationwide marketing. Moreover, many Central European immigrants were tailors and settled in New York to concentrate their talent among Seventh Avenue garment shops.

On the financial side, there were only 613 stocks listed on the NYSE in 1917, and fewer than 500,000 stockholders (there are 42 million stockholders today, of which half are women). Over the years, several brokers and analysts advanced the notion that fashion and finance were somehow related. But we can't relate changes in all of these to the price of stocks. If we used the bikini as a gauge, the DJIA would be propelled to heights previously uncovered (no pun intended)!

Equally, finance covers more than stock prices. It includes: bonds, government securities, bank deposits and loans, mortgages, leaseholds, and mutual funds. Of these financial instruments, stock prices are more publicized, readily measurable, and more responsive to the mood and motion of the economy than any other sector. So we decided to develop a table combining stocks and ladies' hemlines, the most visible and actively followed fashion phenomenon. As a result, we have established a continuing relationship between the two. We are sorry that we couldn't work into our graphics waistlines or necklines, but there was no evidence that plunging necklines and plunging stock markets occur together!

It was easy to get the statistics for stock prices. Hemlines were more difficult, since the styles of many periods referred only to inches above or below the knee. And whose knee? A 6-foot-tall girl would display, at knee length, an entirely different hemline contour than a girl 5 feet 2 inches. So, we selected as standard, a model 5 feet 7 inches tall (equivalent to a size 12 dress). The hemlines depicted are so many inches above the floor so that varying lengths are directly comparable.

Do skirts and stocks go up together? Not quite. If you follow the table for the sixty-two-year period, you'll see that skirts, for the most part, are the lead indicators! They go up before stocks do and ditto on the downside. Hemlines started down ahead of stocks in the 1920–21 depression. Between 1925 and 1926, skirts rose to knee-high, a daring level by historical standards!

The most significant directional guidance to later stock-market action was in 1927 when skirts (in the Flapper era)

BULL MARKETS AND BARE KNEES!
The Hemline Index of Stock Prices

YEAR		INCHES HEM TO FLOOR	DOW JONES INDUSTRIALS MEDIAN
1922		6.4	91
1927	Hemline Peak	18.6	178
1932	Depression	9.8	65
1940–45	War Years	14.5*	140*
1947	Postwar, Dior	8.1	175
1955	Rising Trend	11.6	438
1967	Miniskirt	25.0	857
1978	Maxiskirt	15.0	825
1982	Miniskirt	24.3	924
1983	Consolidation	21.0	1157
1984	Miniskirt	24.0	1187

*Average.

reached new highs (or new thighs). Late in 1927 they started to decline. The year 1927 was a happy one: wide prosperity, animated speakeasies, the Charleston, introduction of the Chrysler car, and stocks in a powerful upthrust. If only the hemline table had been understood and given its message at that time, investors would have known that dreary days for stocks were ahead and saved billions! The downtrend in hemlines preshadowed the market debacle of 1929 by almost two years.

Beginning in late 1932 and pausing to correspond with the slowdown in 1936–37, hemlines began to rise, reaching 8 inches above the ground in 1939 and the **ogling level** of 15 inches in 1940, indicating a market top. World War II followed next, with style sublimated to overalls and jeans for factory work and war production. Ladies' fashions and the stock markets were both on the sidelines during the war.

The wartime skirtline was determined at fairly short levels for two reasons. One, women riding on buses and working at benches or assembly lines did not want long skirts impeding mobility; also, shorter skirts were less likely to get caught in machinery. Second, government restrictions on the production of cloth for civilians limited the mode to garments containing 3½ yards and skirt widths to 64 inches. Fashion was virtually frozen for five years.

Everyone expected a depression after World War II, and hemlines were lower in 1947 than on VJ Day. These lower skirts foretold quite well the descending stock market of 1949.

The 1950s witnessed a general rise in the DJIA (checked in 1953) and again in 1956. The long dress of 1950–51 gave place to rising hemlines, especially notable in 1954. In October 1961, skirts were close to knee-high again, which gave warning to investors that the dip, ten months later, was only a lull, not the end of the bull market. Thus, skirts continued to rise and topped off with the miniskirt, which surfaced about the time the DJIA reached an all-time closing high of 1001 on February 9, 1966.

Some decline in skirt lengths in 1970–71, presaged the sell-off in 1974. Beginning in 1975, there was a slow rise in hemlines, with the height greatest in 1979 foretelling a closing DJIA that reached 1031 in November 1980.

Thus, the chronology of hemlines documented a significant relationship between skirts and stocks. But what's the motivation? Both market swings and fashion changes are fueled as much by emotions as by money logic. High stocks and high skirts seem to reflect confidence, exuberance, hope, and happiness. Good times tend to spark amorous zeal, more animated girl watching, and this watching seems more pleasurable if there is "more girl" to look at! The sex drive and the money drive may originate from the same emotional sources. Stock dividends are more animating than margin calls! In developed nations, birth rates rise during prosperity and fall during depressions. Perhaps, too, the fashion trend toward lower skirts is a form of economic discipline tending to make men pay more attention to business when it is less prosperous!

Another observable phenomenon is that higher skirts, symbolizing hope, confidence, and zest are linked emotionally to livelier colors. The miniskirts of 1966–67 featured a dazzling array of sporty colors—pastels, pinks, reds, yellows, and purples.

If psychological spurs can be found in rising skirt levels, perhaps also zesty attitudes can be reversed by longer skirts, cooling down romantic enthusiasm and ardor. Longer skirts are usually heavier and in darker colors: browns, dark grays, and blacks. In 1932 skirts were not only long, but somber and funereal in color.

The constant emotional urge for a change both in financial and apparel fashions may rationalize the relationship we have tried to establish between hemline and market heights—between sex and stocks. We think our table is of some value as a barometer or cross check on the market motions, and we are particularly impressed that the top of the hemlines in 1967, 28 inches off the ground, so clearly heralded a coming peak in stock prices.

We rest our case on the general theory that hemlines precede in their motion and direction, the rise or fall of common stocks. Sort of a peek and valley formula! In any event, higher skirts appear to be a leading indicator that the time to sell is coming.

Since 1978 to present, hemlines have been rising and presently threaten the former all-time thigh-high of the late sixties, the microskirt hemlines. Similarly, the market has been strong on record volume. Who knows where stocks will go if skirts get shorter? And how shall we chart the correlation with a Dow of 2000? By a navel engagement? A sound market slogan would seem to be: "Don't sell till you see the heights of their thighs!"

Glossary

Accumulation The earliest phase in a bull market. A significant uptrend.

American Stock Exchange The second major stock exchange in the United States.

Analyst An investment professional who evaluates securities and market trends.

Annual Report The official statement and summary of assets, liabilities, earnings, and net worth and progress (if any), of a company covering a fiscal or calendar year.

Average Any one of the various barometers of stock-price trends. Best known are the Dow Jones Industrial Average; the *New York Times* Average of fifty stocks; Standard & Poor's Average of 425 stocks; and the New York Stock Exchange Common Stock Index, a composite of all listed common stocks.

Balance Sheet A financial statement defining the assets, liabilities, capital, and net worth of a corporation on a specified date.

Bear One who believes the market is going down, and who may sell stock "short" to back up his opinions.

Blue Chip Stock Common stock of a major company with a long record of earnings and dividends.

Bond Long-term interest-bearing obligation of a company to repay a given sum (usually $1,000 denomination) on a given date, with a specified rate of interest to be paid at regular intervals until then. A bond can be a debenture, or protected by collateral, lien, or mortgage on corporate property.

151

Broker A security dealer associated with a member of a stock exchange or a broker/dealer firm who executes buy and sell orders for a commission.

Bull One who believes the stock market will rise, and aims to profit if it does.

Capital Asset Land, factories, equipment, or transport equipment owned by a company.

Capital Gain The profit resulting from selling a security for a higher net price than paid.

Capitalization The total of all securities (debt and equity) issued by a company.

Chicago Board of Exchange The exchange on which most options are traded.

Commission The fee charged by a broker for execution of an order to buy or sell.

Common Stock The ownership or equity interest in a corporation with a claim on assets or earnings, coming after the deduction of debt and preferred stock (if any).

Debenture The long-term unsecured obligation of a corporation.

Delisting When a security is removed from trading on a stock exchange and reverts to the OTC market.

Discount Rate The percentage charged by the Federal Reserve Bank on loans to its member banks.

Distribution The cresting phase of a bull market. Time to sell!

Dividend A payment authorized by the board of directors of a corporation, either in cash or stock, pro rata among shareholders. Usually a distribution made from current or past profits.

Dow Jones Industrial Average (DJIA) The combined price index of stocks for thirty of the most important corporations in the United States.

Equity The interest in a company represented by shares of its common or preferred stocks.

Federal Reserve Board The governing body of the Federal Reserve System and the quasi-governmental agency controlling the supply and price of money and regulating installment credit and margin loans.

Going Public   Bringing the securities of a company to market by a public offering at a designated price.

Insider   Technically, anyone owning more than five percent of a company's stocks.

Institutional Investing   Purchase and sale of securities by mutual, endowment or pension funds, banks, and insurance companies.

Interest   The price or rental paid for the use of money, usually stated in per annum percentages.

IRA   Investment Retirement Account. A tax-sheltered plan permitting deductions (up to $2,000 annually) to build a retirement income at age 59 or later.

Junk Bond   High-yielding bond rated BB or below by Standard and Poor's.

Keogh   Tax-sheltered plan for self-employed people to build up a pension fund for retirement.

Leveraged Buying   Using other people's money to generate earnings or gain for you, as when large amounts of senior securities exist in a corporate capitalization, ahead of its common stock. Leverage is also created by using borrowed money to buy stocks or a house with a mortgage.

Liquidation   Nervous selling by those who overstayed a bull market.

Listing   Scheduling corporation securities for trading on an exchange.

Margin   The sum of money or value of securities actually deposited with a broker to purchase securities. Margin requirements (currently 50 percent of the cost of securities purchased) are determined at intervals by the Federal Reserve Board. Margin purchase is designed to enable a person to buy more securities than his own resources would permit.

Margin Call   A broker's request to put up more money or collateral to protect security holdings that have declined and that were purchased in part on borrowed money.

Markup   The aggressive bidding up of prices in the second phase of a bull market.

154   *Glossary*

New Issue   Initial public offering of a security.
New York Stock Exchange   The major stock exchange in the United States.

Operation Baitback   A procedure whereby, if a stock has gained 150 percent you sell half the stock and keep the remaining half. The cost of the stock is then nothing, after payment of all taxes, transfer, or brokerage charges. It prevents paper profits from melting away.
Outstanding Stock   Security issued and in public hands.
Over-the-Counter   The largest nationwide telephone and electronic market for those securities not regularly listed or traded on an exchange.

Penny Stock   Speculative issue selling below $1.
Preferred Stock   An issue of stock having a claim on assets and dividends of a corporation, ahead of the common stock, and usually entitled to dividends at a fixed rate.
Premium   Usually the amount by which a new security sells above its issue price, or a bond above its denomination.
Price/Earnings Ratio (P/E)   The current price of a stock divided by the per-share net earnings of a company for the most recent twelve-month period.
Principal   A dealer who buys and sells securities for his own account.

Quotation   An indication of the market value of a security by naming bid and asked prices.

Security   A generic term for all marketable financial instruments.
Selling Short   Offering for sale a security you do not own.
Sell-Off   Sharp decline in share prices either denoting a pause or the end in a bull market.
Share   A certificate representing a fractional ownership interest in a corporation.
Speculation   The purchase of an asset for gain rather than income.
Stock Dividend   A dividend paid in stock rather than in cash.
Stock Split   Increasing the number of outstanding shares in a company by dividing the existing ones.
Stock   Certificate evidencing ownership in the equity of a company.

Sweetener Something added in a new offering or reorganization plan to make a security more attractive; usually, a warrant or a conversion privilege.

Thin Market One in which trading is infrequent with inside spreads between bid and asked prices.

Underwriter Investment firm offering an issue of securities to the public.

Warrants The right to buy a share or fractional shares of a company's stock at a stated price and within a specified time limit. The subscription price is what you must pay to buy the shares, and the termination date is when the privilege expires.

Index

So, if you bought $100,000 of S&P in Feb. If I bel. the bottom cd. fall out, I cd use S&P os insurance & if I did, then I cd leave $ in great stocks like the dozens of great little companies I cd be in & they cd now be collapsed. I cd ho. stored liquid in

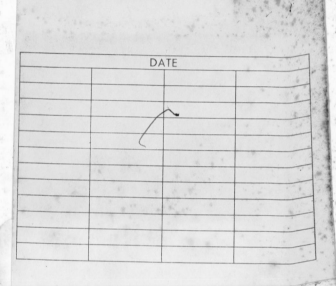